Being
SAGE

To Our Grandchildren and All Their Offspring

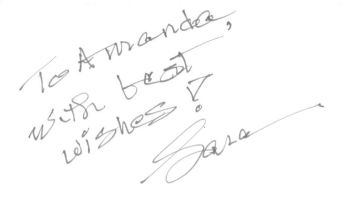

To Amanda,
with best
wishes!
Sara

Being
SAGE

Memories of the
First 45 Years

Sara Miller McCune

For information:

SAGE Publications, Inc.
2455 Teller Road
Thousand Oaks,
    California 91320
E-mail: order@sagepub.com

SAGE Publications India Pvt. Ltd
B 1/I 1 Mohan Cooperative
    Industrial Area
Mathura Road, New Delhi 110 044
India

SAGE Publications Ltd
1 Oliver's Yard
55 City Road
London EC1Y 1SP
United Kingdom

SAGE Publications Asia-Pacific Pte. Ltd
33 Pekin Street #02-01
Far East Square
Singapore 048763

Printed in the United States of America

Library of Congress Cataloging-in-Publication Data

McCune, Sara Miller.
Being SAGE: memories of the first 45 years / Sara Miller McCune.
    p. cm.
Includes index.
ISBN 978-1-4129-8909-1 (acid-free paper)
    1. Sage Publications, inc.—History. 2. Publishers and publishing—History—20th century. 3. Publishers and publishing—History—21st century. 4. McCune, Sara Miller. 5. Publishers and publishing—California—Biography. I. Title.

Z473.S23M33 2010
070.509794′94—dc22   2010008357

This book is printed on acid-free paper.

10   11   12   13   14   10   9   8   7   6   5   4   3   2   1

Production Editor:	Astrid Virding
Copy Editor:	Gillian Dickens
Typesetter:	C&M Digitals (P) Ltd
Proofreader:	Scott Oney
Indexer:	Molly Hall
Cover Designer:	Ravi Balasuriya

Contents

Part IV. The Millennium and Beyond

Preface

Overall, the events of this book flow chronologically from the beginning of SAGE's history to a conclusion in the present time. However, the subjects I cover have at times required, for the sake of coherence, that I tell the full story up to the present, jumping ahead a bit in the chronology. The book is designed in this way so if readers wish, they can delve into a particular subject to see its development over time without having to search in a future chapter for more of the story.

However, for those topics where I have followed a chronological order, dividing some developments between chapters in telling the story, I provide cross-references to help the reader find a continuation of information.

Acknowledgments

In this book, I have combined many different perspectives to tell the story of SAGE, although I am the overall author, and I take full responsibility for any inaccuracies.

I want to acknowledge with gratitude those who provided their words as text and so were actually co-authors for this book. For that help, I wish to especially thank the following: Blaise Simqu (Chapter 11), David F. McCune (Chapter 10), Stephen Barr (Chapters 9 and 11), Ziyad Marar (Chapter 9), and Matt Jackson (Chapter 4), whose voices join mine in this book to tell the story of SAGE. The editor who worked with us, Nancy Marriott, should also take a deep bow and perhaps a sigh of relief.

I want to thank all those who gave their time for interviews and provided their valuable memories or perspectives, including Marilyn Gittell, Jon Goodman, Claudia Armann, Sandra Ball-Rokeach, Geane De Lima, Michael Todd, and John Mecklin.

I am, as always, extremely grateful to a number of people at SAGE Publications, Inc. who made the job of writing (and in some cases, rewriting) this book much easier than it ought to have been. Several of them (especially Kate Wilde and Paula Green) make my entire life easier and better than I probably deserve! Karen Bordonaro, Kim Lyman, Roberta Isaeff, Martha Zeiher, Alison Mudditt, Carolyn Crandall, Rolf Janke, Jayne Marks, and Sara van Valkenburg were there whenever needed for two solid months. Kate Wilde, who has been with me in her capacity as Executive Assistant for over 15 years, has been—and continues to be—amazing. Her assistant, Paula Green, is due a party on her one-year anniversary with us while this book is in the final stages of printing. We plan to make sure the luncheon celebrating her arrival on the SAGE scene is celebrated in appropriate style.

In addition, I want to acknowledge three invaluable sources that were excerpted and/or adapted with permission by the author or publisher:

Kathleen Reardon and Victoria Whiting for their 1994 article, "Strategic Alliance in India: Sage Publications," in R. T. Moran, D. O. Braaten, & J. E. Walsh Jr. (Eds.), *International Business Case Studies for the Multicultural Marketplace,* p. 5, as published by Gulf Publishing Company, Houston, TX, and copyright © 1994 by Elsevier (used in Chapters 4 and 8); John W. Creswell from his report in the 2009 SAGE published book, *How SAGE Has Shaped Research Methods: A 40-Year History* (used in Chapters 3 and 5); and Matthew Jackson for material from his privately published memoir, *Not Only a Grandpa,* in 2002 (used in Chapter 4).

And finally, I wish to acknowledge and thank the many people who contributed to the SAGE publication *A Celebration in Words: SAGE 1965–2005,* whose words I have excerpted in condensed vignettes and testimonials throughout this book.

PART I

In the Beginning . . .

CHAPTER 1

A Publishing Company
of One's Own

SAGE Publications, Inc. was incorporated in early January 1965 in New York City, just one month before my 24th birthday. When I founded the company, I'd had 3½ years of experience in the publishing business, first at Macmillan, Inc. in New York and subsequently at Pergamon Press, Ltd in Oxford, England. It was a bold step that quickly grew into a mission, which has been to publish thoughtful works of scholarship by and for educators, authors, and other scholars throughout the world.

A Natural Choice

My choice to go solo was based in many things. For one, I had become disenchanted with large-scale publishing houses. Both Macmillan (and the Free Press), which had been absorbed and merged into a subsumed entity by Crowell-Collier a few months before I joined them in late June 1961, and Pergamon, then being driven on the first of its massive growth quests by the legendary Robert Maxwell, had more than a thousand employees each. Everywhere I turned during my first years in the book industry, I saw examples of what not to do.

Another factor influencing my choice to start my own company was that, growing up, I took for granted having a high level of self-confidence. I was used to thinking I could do anything I chose to do or wanted to do. I had traveled around the United States and Canada, making speeches for a youth group that I belonged to from age 15 until I was 19. I had worked on a newspaper, written articles, acted a bit in plays and on television professionally—not very well—but what was important is that I had a sense I could do all of these things, and I did them.

Because I was able and fortunate to skip a grade in junior high in the New York City school system, I found myself graduating high school four months after my 16th birthday. I had won a New York State Regents Scholarship and used it to attend Queens College of the City University of New York (CUNY), graduating at the early age of 20. As a result, for the next decade or so, I wound up being the youngest person in practically every endeavor I undertook. I can remember, having started SAGE in my mid-20s, discovering at the ripe old age (to me) of 28 that we had signed a 26-year-old author, meaning I was no longer "the youngest." I had an awful crisis in thinking that I was getting old and then realized maybe I wasn't quite *that* old. I would, no doubt, feel much older later on in life, as indeed has come to pass, but at the time, no longer being younger than everyone around me was a startling realization and took some getting used to.

But back then, when I was growing up, it never crossed my mind that if there was something I truly wanted to do, I wouldn't be able to do it and be reasonably good at it. I knew I wasn't a particularly good swimmer; I knew I was never going to win bridge tournaments, because I wasn't very good at playing bridge. But the things I cared about and wanted to do, like travel, I somehow figured out a way to do. With this being my mind-set, I didn't have any great anxiety about starting a business. I thought about it, and I knew I didn't have very much to risk. It seemed like a natural step for me.

The source of my earliest self-confidence involves a bit of family history. I was the oldest child in my family; my brother is five years younger than I am. On my father's side, his generation of siblings consisted of four brothers, all of whom had their own businesses, small or medium sized. One of my father's brothers was a lawyer, who eventually devoted his career to real estate holdings. Another was a successful principal of a high-quality stationery and greeting card enterprise. My father had a small business, and his younger brother opened and ran two retail businesses in succession. Very simply, I absorbed from my father's side of the family the notion that it was perfectly normal to have your own business. All sorts of people had their own businesses, and there was no big deal about it.

My mother's side had the exact opposite profile, being people who preferred employment in the businesses of others. However, I don't recall thinking there was any difference between my uncles who had their own businesses and the uncle on my mother's side who became an accountant and a partner in a large and prestigious accounting firm. I didn't consciously make the distinction that it was better to have your own business and be self-employed. It simply seemed the ordinary thing to do.

Influence of George D. McCune

In addition to having a naturally confident outlook and a family model of entrepreneurship, I was encouraged in my publishing pursuits by the man who subsequently became my husband, George D. McCune. George had been my second boss and mentor at Macmillan, Inc. (in New York City), where I'd had my first job out of college. George envied my freedom to take the risk of starting my own imprint after only a short time (and three rapid promotions) in the industry and encouraged me to do so. He was the only one. My family thought I should marry and have kids!

George's contacts at Macmillan, especially with a man named Jeremiah (Jerry) Kaplan, positioned us both in a unique way, even before I had thought of starting my own publishing company, to enter an area that would bear immense fruit for SAGE and the world. How that all came about is worth a short digression to fill in some of the background on SAGE's impact on scholarly publishing and the development of academic research in the last half of the 20th century.

The story begins with George's association with Jerry Kaplan, the founder of the Free Press, which was the first preeminent social science imprint in the United States. The Free Press was acquired and merged with Macmillan when Crowell-Collier bought both firms in 1961. As a result, George, who worked for Macmillan at the time, and Jerry became close colleagues. They worked very well together, although they were quite different in background, personality, and life experience. However, both were visionaries.

Jerry was a brilliant man who had done a lot of co-publishing with educational publishers throughout the UK (especially Routledge in London). The first translations of Durkheim and Weber and many other great names in

European social science appeared in the United States under the Free Press imprint—the company that, once subsumed into Macmillan, Jerry continued to watch over.

George's career at Macmillan spanned his beginning position in the College Division (where he worked himself up from salesman to second in command) to his becoming Vice President for Sales (with four of Macmillan's seven sales departments reporting to him). When Crowell-Collier bought the Free Press, they moved it from the Chicago area and merged it into Macmillan in New York; shortly thereafter, Jerry was promoted to Executive Vice President of Macmillan. (Jerry ultimately became president of Macmillan and was promoted by Crowell-Collier several years later to shape up Collier-Macmillan, Ltd, their international operations based in London.)

About two years later, in 1963, George became Director of the Free Press, promoted to this position by Jerry Kaplan, to watch over and grow his first-born imprint. One of the first things George did was launch the Free Press paperbacks, a series with, initially, four dozen Free Press classics. All were in an affordable price range; a teaching assistant or junior faculty member or serious advanced undergraduate could easily select from them to build the backbone of a generation's professional library in sociology or political science.

George and I met at Macmillan in late 1961. I had three different jobs before I started working for myself in 1965, two at Macmillan between 1961 and 1963 and one at Pergamon Press, Ltd in Oxford, England, for one year starting from the spring of 1963. I went to work at Pergamon because it was a good career opportunity (and I loved England). I'd never been there before, but I was already an Anglophile.

There were other forces behind my move that had to do with the restructuring going on in the publishing industry at the time. Today I can look back on many rounds of what I call "merger mania," a trend that started shortly after I began working in publishing in mid-1961 and spread across the ocean from the United States and Canada to the UK. We saw firsthand what big mergers do to an imprint and how inevitably, within a few years, the editorial focus at the heart of one imprint after another succumbed to the lawyers, the accountants, the number crunchers, the analysts, the Wall Street people. One after another of the most ambitious, caring, passionate, and talented individuals who experienced this change chose to leave the industry and start their own companies, including myself and another of my colleagues (with a background from Prentice-Hall), Allan Jossey-Bass, who also started his own company in 1965. There were several others we knew who were part of this trend, on both sides of the Atlantic.

To ensure such events can never happen to SAGE, George and I set up our estate plan so that SAGE cannot be sold unless the outside directors find it has lost money for two years in a row, which we have not done in three and a half decades (even when there was a recession during Nixon's presidency), and the directors cannot see, in some new environment that we don't yet know about (beyond digital publishing), a way of turning it around. As a result of our commitment to independence, the most talented people in the world of publishing come to us to see if we have openings and end up staying for long careers. This plan is still something that I watch over regularly, revising and updating as necessary.

But back to my story. In late 1962, Macmillan acquired the distribution rights in North and South America to Pergamon's book list (not the journals, which was their real moneymaker). The deal was made at the Frankfurt Book Fair in Germany by Robert Maxwell, who had founded Pergamon and was still running it. Macmillan acquired the distribution rights largely because Warren Sullivan (then Macmillan's president) had been a publisher at John Wiley & Sons and wanted a scientific and technical list, which had been a great success at Wiley. Elsevier and other European publishers had also found STM (science, technology, and medicine) to be very lucrative.

Because Pergamon was publishing scientific and technical books and journals, Maxwell was very taken with some of the things that George and I, as part of Macmillan's sales team, had developed for the Pergamon book list. At Macmillan, we had never sold scientific books prior to acquiring Pergamon's titles, and our salesmen couldn't even pronounce the names of the authors, much less pronounce the titles or subjects. I put together various sales packages (and George was generous enough to tell Maxwell that I had been a prime mover in that), and the sales managers had also figured out a way to use Plexiglas bookstands for display in the bookstores, so that the sales staff could sell to the major bookstores carrying scientific and medical books and be competitive in the big bookstores.

At the time, the region covering the Chicago area and the Midwest was like the state of Massachusetts in the East, populated by major universities that had significant medical schools and large science and engineering programs, and Macmillan was now aiming to sell to the big bookstores in that area. There were still many large independent stores then, as opposed to now. Kroch's & Brentano's, the largest bookstore in Chicago and at one time the largest privately owned bookstore chain in the United States, closed in 1995. But at that time, in the early 1960s, Kroch's & Brentano's was a major retail player in selling STM books.

Macmillan's salesmen had been good at selling mysteries, westerns, gardening books, children's books, religious books, with great authors like C. S. Lewis (who also wrote children's books), and more general books like *Gone With the Wind* (which saved the company from going bankrupt during the Depression), but they weren't oriented toward STM books. When Macmillan picked up Pergamon's book list, the sales force had to be trained and encouraged in order to sell these types of books effectively by placing them in the appropriate retail and wholesale outlets, enabling them to reach libraries, and so forth. This effort and its follow-ups taught me much about marketing specialized lists and targeting niche distribution outlets—knowledge I would use later to build my own company and, at the same time, help to establish new fields and specializations in the social sciences.

With George's contacts through Jerry Kaplan and the Free Press, on my return from England I was ready to start my own publishing company; we were poised to become important players—even "gatekeepers"—in what was then a major branching of the fields of sociology and political science, taking us into a multitude of new fields that would very significantly impact the future.

And so SAGE Publications was born in January 1965. My parents at the time were hoping for my marriage, preferably to a nice Jewish doctor or lawyer, and for at least two grandchildren. My friends in publishing thought I might perhaps be too young and inexperienced—a month before my 24th birthday—to start my own company. But I had nothing to risk and everything to gain.

First SAGE Publication

My first step was to hunt down a former college classmate who was an attorney and have him set up a corporation. My start-up capital was $500, half of which came from the value of a used air conditioner. I did some consulting with other small publishing firms in New York City, to bring in some much needed revenue, and I began networking—seeking ideas to grow the company.

With so little start-up capital, I clearly needed to publish or sell things that would bring me positive cash flow from day one. George was a behind-the-scenes brainstorming presence at that point, while retaining his position as a Vice President at Macmillan. After considering the possibility of starting a social science book club, the merits of starting with a journal and publishing a booklist around it quickly took on great appeal.

On the evening of the day I was informed that my corporate charter had been granted, I was having drinks with my former mentor and political science professor at Queens College, Marilyn Gittell. Marilyn was my teacher, my mentor, my boss. In turn, I was her student, babysitter, boss (for a brief but memorable time), publishing partner-in-crime, editorial adviser, friend, fellow board member (on various occasions, including currently), and often unindicted co-conspirator!

A political scientist who had graduated from Brooklyn College, Marilyn was my most compelling political science professor at Queens College, part of a small but strong (and mostly terrific and accomplished) group of professors, including a few seasoned government professionals. The Department Chair at Queens had been a running mate of legendary New York City Mayor Fiorello LaGuardia (and Dr. McGoldrick never let us forget it!). Al Castagno, who taught us the basics of foreign policy, had advised JFK's transitional team on Africa. Mary Earhart Dillon (sister of the tragic Amelia) taught the introductory course in American government.

Marilyn herself was a brilliant, forceful, and outspoken expert on state and local government. Years later, when I was in London with my husband and had to step over splitting bags of uncollected refuse in the SoHo district—a victim (with millions of others) of labor unrest at the time—I remember telling George that Marilyn's fervor about city government included the importance of garbage collection!

On that evening in 1965 over drinks, Marilyn was lamenting the fact that the City University of New York had no university press, and therefore there was no logical home for a journal she wanted to start called *Urban Affairs Quarterly*. Maybe it was the scotch (although I prefer to think it was fate and the recognition of an exciting potential opportunity), but I immediately offered to publish the journal through my new company, and my offer was accepted the next day. George was there, encouraging us, as was Marilyn's husband, Irwin Gittell, who agreed to become the company's first accountant.

The founding editor of the first journal SAGE published (*Urban Affairs Quarterly,* now *Urban Affairs Review*), Marilyn was until her death on February 26, 2010, doing research and mentoring graduate students at the City University of New York. A truly inspiring and accomplished scholar, she was the Director of the Samuels Center at CUNY, a member of the McCune Foundation Board of Directors, a fiendish tennis player, and an insightful friend.

Getting off the Ground

At that point, I was SAGE's sole employee. I had a one-room office at 150 Fifth Avenue at the corner of 20th Street, a location that was the birthplace of several publishing companies. I was at the north end of Manhattan's traditional publishing and bookselling enclaves and just south of the toy district. By day, I worked at least three days a week at other small publishing clients' offices, and by night (and every other spare minute I could find), I'd be at SAGE's office. I did the copyediting and proofreading, watched the typesetting forms being locked up, and smelled the ink as the first issue of *UAQ* rolled off the letterpress in September 1965. (Before offset printing was developed, from the 1600s or earlier until the late 20th century, typesetters would put the words into print by hand.) Similar to producing a baby, it took nine months for SAGE to birth its first journal.

Long before that first issue rolled off the press, however, I was traveling around the United States, gathering mailing lists of urban affairs specialists, getting as many names as possible for free. I also was introducing myself to social scientists in this and related fields, scouting for books and other periodical products to publish, especially in sociology and politics.

At night, between June and September of that first year, I typed addresses from my mailing lists onto a one-page self-mailer to try to generate subscriptions for *UAQ*. At first, I could only afford to mail 500 at a time, licking the 4-cent stamps myself. But as the $12 checks came in, I was able to do a second mailing to all 3,600 names with the help of a retired gentleman (wanting to augment his Social Security pension) and a wet sponge. Even so, the taste of stamp glue still makes my stomach cramp to this day!

The response was excellent, and SAGE had learned its first lesson about the effectiveness of highly targeted direct mail. By the time the first issue of *UAQ* was printed, we had sold enough subscriptions to pay the printer. A second valuable lesson had been learned in cash flow management, which was to sell subscriptions in advance in order to bring in enough money to print, market, and mail—and, eventually, pay rent and salaries, too. Neither lesson was ever forgotten.

By the end of its first year, SAGE not only had successfully launched *Urban Affairs Quarterly* but also had announced the imminent publication of the first volume in a companion annual series, *Urban Research and Policy Planning,* Volume 1 of the *Urban Affairs Annual Reviews.* We had also acquired our second journal, *American Behavioral Scientist,* from Al De Grazia, the academic who co-founded it in 1957. He had hired me as a marketing consultant in 1964 and then poured all new and renewal subscription revenues into an ill-fated and costly computerized information retrieval service in political science. When his debts overwhelmed him in the fall of 1965, I acquired *American Behavioral Scientist* in exchange for assuming the bulk of his indebtedness. The information retrieval service no longer exists. I am happy to report that *American Behavioral Scientist,* however, still thrives as one of SAGE's flagship journals.

After deciding to acquire *American Behavioral Scientist,* I went to my paternal grandmother and asked for a loan, which she gave me. It was money that was supposed to go to my father and my uncles as a holiday present, so I paid them each back over four years with interest, and I never looked back.

CHAPTER 2

Westward Ho!

In the winter of 1966, I visited both Chicago and California. In Chicago, I started the process of networking intensively on behalf of SAGE—looking up former Free Press authors introduced to me by James S. Coleman, Peter Rossi, or Morris Janowitz. All were scholars George knew (or I knew of) from Chicago days who were disillusioned by the post-merger Free Press. Having worked at Macmillan shortly after that wave of "merger mania," I was aware of the unhappiness of many social scientists about the changes in the Free Press. It was the first time SAGE ever exploited the post-merger blues—and given subsequent outbreaks of merger madness, the skills learned were certainly put to good use, both by myself and, later, by other SAGE editors as well. (See Chapter 6 for more on our development of contacts in the Midwest.) In California, I networked with people in the field of urban studies at UCLA, USC, and UC Berkeley.

Meanwhile, George was becoming restless. Having decided he could no longer work for Macmillan (or any other giant corporation over whose policies he did not exert control) and that he never wanted to work in New York City again—and also having decided to file for divorce—he set about convincing me to marry him, which wasn't very hard, and to move SAGE to California. The latter was the more difficult proposition!

For a New Yorker like me, the decision to relocate our SAGE office from New York City to California was not an easy one. SAGE had been incorporated in New York City by a real New Yorker—one born, raised, and educated there. Despite extensive travel in the United States and Canada, and working in England and on the Continent, my mental map of the country rather mirrored *The New Yorker* magazine's mocking cover portrayal of the United States, showing New York as huge, Florida as conspicuous, California dwarfed by Hollywood, and most of the Midwest as nonexistent.

But by then, the question was, if SAGE moves to California, should it be Northern or Southern California? Despite George's not-so-secret preference for the San Francisco Bay Area and the incredible hospitality of the School of Environmental Design at UC Berkeley (forever dear to my heart!), I must admit I was influenced by crass considerations, such as the weather and other things that best come under the heading of "the mechanics of living." Probably the key example of this was learning to drive. As a New Yorker, I'd never needed to get a driver's license, and in England, I also did without, after seeing them all drive on the wrong side of the road! San Francisco didn't appear to be that much better for a first-time driver, with its steep, twisting streets looming frighteningly around every corner.

The decision was made: SAGE would move to Southern California. By June 1966, an office was rented in Beverly Hills; by July, I had moved out to California with two relatively new but loyal support staffers; and by October, George and I were married. My parents, who'd expected me to marry a Jewish man, said they would come to the wedding if a rabbi officiated. So George found the only rabbi in Southern California who was willing to marry us, and we had a traditional ceremony on October 16. We started married life in our new home, an apartment near SAGE's recently rented offices in Beverly Hills.

In California, SAGE had four employees (including George and myself), more space, two more periodicals in the works, the beginnings of a book publishing program, and the start of a whole new era in the company's publishing philosophy. The end of the 1960s was to bring us into other disciplines and fields, as well as see us searching for capital to expand the company and take us in two important publishing directions: the innovative publication of SAGE Papers and the decision to cross the pond to England (see Chapters 3 and 4).

Early Fiscal Growth

The move to California was marked by an upsurge in sales and growth. Back in New York, sales during our first fiscal year (1965) had been a minuscule $12K. I can remember the fiscal year of 1965/66 being in the range of $40K.

The first year in California (a truncated seven-month period from June 1, 1966, through the end of December) saw sales grow to nearly $100K, as we moved from a business based on selling consulting services (mine) to one based on selling real products (two journals and two book series).

The first year was so paltry because that amount consisted almost totally of consulting fees, allowing me to keep myself alive while gathering and preparing manuscripts to publish. But from 1967 on, we focused a great deal on growth, and because we were so small back then, it was easy to double our revenues (and most of the time, our profits as well) for many years in a row. From 1967 through 1969, we'd grown 265%. In the 1970s, we grew to be almost 8.5 times larger. In the 1980s, we went up almost 300%. During the 1990s, profits for the group grew from just over $1.6 million a year to about $8.5 million a year (a growth in profits of more than five times in ten years). Sales of the group had grown from well under $20 million to nearly $70 million during that decade.

Early on, George and I figured—once the initial doubling and re-doubling ceased and we started growing by a mere 50% a year—that if we could continue to grow sales at a compounded rate of 15% per annum, SAGE's sales would double every five years. Even when we accounted for recessions and setbacks, we were still reasonably certain we would double our sales (and increase our profits) every seven years. That was one of our main growth objectives, and with the exception of one year (1986), those objectives were achieved!

Expanding Our Horizon

The last half of 1967 saw SAGE publishing in new subfields of sociology and political science, as well as expanding into interdisciplinary subfields, such as law and society, political sociology, and urban education. (For more detail on growth during this period, see Chapter 6.) We continued to expand our list of journals. We also were publishing a biweekly newsletter, *Urban Research News,* and we had spun off a social science bibliographic service from the *American Behavioral Scientist,* called *New Studies in the Social and Behavioral Sciences,* which was compiled into a hardcover series called the *ABS Guides.* This in turn led to a small amount of bibliographic publishing and somewhat crude forms of early database publication, mostly in the fields related to urban studies and local, county, and state government. SAGE also began to form strategic alliances with small, often interdisciplinary societies, publishing in cooperation with the Law and Society Association and the Inter-University Seminar on Armed Forces and Society, for example.

During these early years, we focused on publishing in the fields of urban studies, comparative politics, and policy studies. Meanwhile, friend-ships developed with noted social science scholars such as Donald Campbell, the well-known social psychologist who agreed to serve on the editorial board for the SAGE-acquired journal *American Behavioral Scientist,* and distinguished sociologist James S. Coleman, who helped found the SAGE journal *Simulation & Games* (later renamed *Simulation & Gaming*). These individuals were leaders not only for their pathbreaking research in their respective fields but also because of their major and lasting contributions to social science research methodology.

The *American Behavioral Scientist* also provided SAGE with an entrée into a variety of other new endeavors. We used it to "field test" rela-tionships with new journal editors and new fields before launching journals. For example, *Simulation & Games, Youth & Society, Small Group Behavior,* and *Communication Research* all grew out of early encounters with talented academics who first edited a special issue of *American Behavioral Scientist* and then were invited by us to launch new journals to cope with burgeoning literature in these emerging interdisciplinary subfields.

Our turnaround time was very fast in the late 1960s and early 1970s. I was doing nearly all the editorial acquisition work, handling all marketing via direct mail, conventions, and the occasional book club sale, and supervising production, including our earliest forays into in-house typesetting using IBM's magnetic tape selectric composition systems. George McCune did a bit of acquisition work, especially when conventions piled up and preliminary negotiations were hot and heavy! He also supervised all accounting, finan-cial, administrative, and distribution functions. Together we brainstormed ideas for new products (especially journals and book series), new or related fields to enter, marketing ideas, and publishing priorities.

The decision to publish was often made either in our breakfast nook or over our dining room table—with the SA(ra) and the GE(orge) in SAGE hav-ing achieved a remarkable consensus in a very short time frame as to what we wanted to publish, how we could sell it, and how best to finance expansion through internal growth. The 80- to 100-hour workweeks that all of this entailed seemed to fly past. We were busy, happy, having fun, stressed, and loving just about every minute of it!

In the summer of 1969, however, it was obvious that the number of publishing opportunities open to us far exceeded our capital resources. Loath to slow down our growth, which had taken us from just under $100,000 in turnover during the fiscal year ending May 31, 1967, to just under $250,000 in the fiscal year ending May 31, 1969, we turned instead to a group of outside investors gathered together by the late Marvin Sirot. An expert in investments, Sirot at the time was running an East Coast hedge fund and also did some consulting on investments for a large industrial firm's pension fund. These investors bought convertible debentures, which were bonds that paid interest—in those days, a mere 4%.

In September 1969, this fresh infusion of $100,000 in capital enabled us to sign additional contracts for journals and books and to hire two experienced vice presidents, one for manufacturing and production, Frank Comparato, and one for editorial and marketing, Harry McConnell. Frank opened an office in New York City for us but later moved himself and that office to California—driving the rental truck himself.

This infusion of working capital also enabled us to pursue an idea that George had long been dreaming about—a dream that I shared. For a couple of years, we had been trying hard to develop a vehicle that would enable us to publish works longer than journal articles but shorter than books. Many academics wrote monographs of this length but had few, if any, outlets for them. In some cases, such materials were published as "occasional papers" by various research institutes, often in a mimeographed, 8½ × 11–inch format, stapled. They were poorly marketed, if at all, were difficult and expensive for librarians to catalog and shelve, and generally represented a barrier to the dissemination of much good, sound scholarship in the social and behavioral sciences.

We were about to take a leap that would change all that.

CHAPTER 3

*The Great SAGE Papers Caper
and "Little Green Books"*

For a few years after starting SAGE, we toyed with various ideas that would enable us to solve a problem academics often complained about: finding a format to publish materials longer than journal articles but shorter than books.

These kinds of publications were sometimes called "monographs," since they were typically scholarly works written by a single author. Most often they appeared as occasional papers, frequently published by research institutes of different universities and typified by the phrase "fugitive materials," because they were so difficult to track down. Libraries found them hard to collect, and while they often contained very good materials, distribution and advertising were virtually nil. Furthermore, academics frequently got minimal credit for these works, because it was believed (often correctly) that they were published with little or no peer review to guarantee their scholarly quality.

We were determined to find a solution to this problem, and after several years and many long talks with academics, George and I finally thrashed out all the problems we could foresee. The concept of the *SAGE Professional Papers,* born on yellow pads of paper spread out over our kitchen table, was ready to be implemented.

Source: John W. Creswell from his 2009 SAGE published report, *How SAGE Has Shaped Research Methods: A 40-Year History,* a portion of which was drawn from Sara Miller McCune's article on the "Great SAGE Papers Caper" in the SAGE newsletter.

We began discussions with a group of political scientists and eventually decided to set up four series of *SAGE Professional Papers:* in comparative politics (1971), international studies (1973), American politics, and administrative and policy studies (both started in 1974). Each of these series had a series editor or a pair of co-editors who, just like journal editors, handled the reviewing process. Each series also had a small and distinguished editorial advisory board.

The ground rules for publication in the *SAGE Professional Papers* series were that printed materials must be longer than journal articles (more than 32 printed pages) and shorter than books (96 or fewer printed pages). We launched them with a cover price of $3 apiece in a series, allowing libraries to subscribe to 12 papers per year. The series editors and their boards were responsible for picking out 12 exceptionally good papers each year in their field—the *crème de la crème.*

Then, in the early 1970s, we were offered the opportunity to publish the *Washington Papers* on behalf of the Center for Strategic and International Studies in Washington, D.C. This expanded our range of offerings from solely academic/professional to "SAGE policy papers." Since these titles were both policy and foreign policy oriented, they had a broader audience and a broader readership and were somewhat more successful in sales terms; however, they were also more expensive to produce because of the three-color covers. Various research institutes around the world beseeched us to publish and distribute their occasional papers as well, so the professional paper format was extended to make room for "SAGE research papers"—many in the field of sociology.

We certainly encouraged the editors to pick papers of broad significance rather than narrow topical interest. Despite that, in certain of the series, we did get papers with a narrow focus. While often these were exemplar case study types of materials, they still had minimal sales appeal. The assumption was that we could make each series economically viable by selling these papers on subscription, therefore developing either a subscription or standing order base for them with institutions. We would advertise them widely, but always as a group, so advertising costs for the individual papers were spread among an ever-growing number. By having a peer review system to guarantee quality, and also by having the economies of scale of a fully operating assembly line for production (reducing the costs of typesetting and also the expense of paper, printing, and binding), we would achieve great economies of scale.

Thus, we believed, *SAGE Papers* in each field could be marketed and disseminated well and at a reasonable cost. Doing this would build our credibility among authors, as well as hopefully enabling us to have two or three papers that would sell very well in each year's batch of 12 papers. The idea was that those papers would carry the ones in each series that sold modestly. Selling *very* well meant they would have been sold widely to individuals, as well as libraries, and also picked up as supplemental materials for classroom adoption.

In reality, with many of the series, we were lucky if we got one such "best seller" per year. The best sellers tended to outsell the other titles in the series by three or even five to one, so our initial plan of printing a thousand of each paper and then going back on press and printing more of the best sellers didn't always work out as advantageously as we thought it would.

At the same time, these series were an enormous success among the academic community, who were universally delighted with everything about them. They found the editorial process to be enormously beneficial, frequently getting very good advice for ways of revising and strengthening their materials. The publication process usually went very smoothly, and again, they were delighted to see these works in print rather than mimeographed or photocopied from typescript.

Furthermore, the fact that *SAGE Papers* were bound, even though the spines were very slim, in uniform covers, and then widely marketed via direct mail gave their works a great deal more visibility. Additionally, they were reviewed by prestigious editorial boards, which served as guarantors of quality and prestige within academic circles. Many papers were also reviewed in major academic journals, abstracted by the major disciplinary abstract publications, and often cited by other academics in subsequent works. And the fact that scholars could now find a home for material that was too long to be a journal article but too short for a book, of course, was also enormously convenient and helpful to them. I'm assuming it was also helpful in terms of at least a few tenure decisions.

QASS: *The "Little Green Books"*

As a result of this tremendous critical acclaim and the pressure to publish ever more papers, we were approached by Dr. Eric Uslaner (the author of paper #19 in our American Politics series) in 1976 to start a new *SAGE Papers* series in political science quantitative research methods. George succeeded in convincing Dr. Uslaner that such a series would have to be done for all social science disciplines, not just one. Uslaner ultimately gathered a small working editorial board consisting of three political scientists, one sociologist, and one statistician. Because these papers were designed with a clear pedagogical purpose, they were named *SAGE University Papers,* and that's how the familiar *Quantitative Applications in the Social Sciences (QASS)* series began.

By the summer of 1976, the *QASS* series was under way, quickly becoming a success. Known by social scientists and their students as the "little green books," the papers took their alias from the plain green covers that bore nothing but a title, the author's name, and the name of the series. Iverson and Norpoth's *Analysis of Variance,* Nagel's *Operations Research,* and Henkel's *Tests of Significance* were among the first titles in the series and, at $3 each, met with immediate success.

The papers were highly regarded for both quality and utility, and they sold "like hotcakes," Mitch Allen, our sociology editor, reported. For the first time, we had a *SAGE Papers* series that was a clear and obvious success in financial terms. We developed lists of the top 20 quantitative techniques and then went out and found authors to write short 96-page books on the topics. The "little green books" found use in classrooms, libraries placed standing orders for these books as "sets," and each year we published and printed three groups of four at a time.

Today, in 2010, more than 165 volumes of the "little green books" are in print with titles that reflect the evolution of quantitative methods, from basic statistics, types of data, and measurement to computer applications and gaming. Many books sold well, including the most popular one of them all, Michael Lewis-Beck's *Applied Regression,* published in 1980. I always thought 50 or perhaps 100 titles would cover the statistical universe—but other opinions prevailed. I do remember (with great delight) the party we had at SAGE's office in California to celebrate the sale of one million copies of the various titles (including Series Editor Michael Lewis-Beck's landmark volume on regression analysis).

In the meantime, between 1971 and 1978, the *SAGE Professional Papers* and the *SAGE Research Papers* managed to rack up a loss of approximately $100,000 between them. While each year's loss was small and bearable, we were always convinced that the *next* year would bring a turning point to a least minimally profitable status. Instead, we continued small but steady losses of $10,000 or $15,000 per year. This was at a time when we were trying to expand our book publishing program, launch new journals, publish in new fields, and get SAGE, Ltd in London up and running. So with a great deal of reluctance, all but the *University Papers* were discontinued in 1981 with an enormous sale of old inventory since there were over 100 titles in print. There was always deep regret on our part and within the academic community that we had not been able to make this noble idea a moneymaker.

There were several lessons that we learned by applying 20–20 hindsight to the process. Certainly the success of the *University Papers,* as compared with the difficulties experienced with the professional papers and the research papers, suggested that although very good things could indeed come in small packages, they needed to be developed in subject areas that could sell across multiple fields in the social sciences.

And so the subsequent series that were developed, such as the *Qualitative Research Methods Series* (*QRMs*) and the *Applied Social Research Methods Series* (*ASRMs*) (which were slightly longer, i.e., 128 to 160 printed pages), were indeed developed in the areas of social research methodology that could sell across multiple disciplines and therefore easily produced more successes per each group of, say, 10 or 12 papers published. The higher ratio of success, the higher percentages of classroom adoption, and the greater ease of selling packages (multiple titles to a single customer on each invoice) made the entire process much more economically viable while still being fairly successful in the authors' terms.

What we have not been able to figure out, despite the considerable amount of lengthy postmortem sessions over many a dinner and a cup of coffee or a friendly drink with an astonishing variety of social scientists who have never ceased to mourn the demise of the *SAGE Professional Papers,* is how to make this format viable within a single discipline or subdiscipline and within a small subject area niche. Even the demise of a methodology series in the field of geography in the mid-1980s pointed again to the difficulty of doing this across too small a base of potential customers.

In sum, the lessons learned include these: (1) Good things often come in small packages, (2) the marketplace being served needs to be broad enough to appeal across disciplines, and (3) the series that were and are most successful need to appeal not only to academics seeking a brush-up or to enhance knowledge on a specific topic but also to multiple generations of majors and graduate students in a variety of fields.

It is clear that these papers are prized by academics and are also among the most desired and best utilized items in current use by generations of social science students who have been weaned on papers in modular publications in various fields of research methodology.

PART II

*Taking Risks and
Growing a Legacy*

CHAPTER 4

Crossing the Pond

London in 1971

Three years after we had reincorporated in Beverly Hills, California, George and I took on $100,000 in debt from outside investors (in 1969). This financial deal (subsequently repaid with considerable interest) provided the seed money for us to achieve our vision of amplifying the voices of academics and having them heard around the world. SAGE's first step into the global business environment was a 1971 move to London.

The decision to set up a SAGE counterpart in London was either brave or foolhardy, depending on how one looked at it. In 1971, when SAGE, Inc. was a bit more than seven years old, we had a turnover of less than a million dollars annually, and to use the cash flow to build our first international publishing affiliate was unusual, to say the least. Most American businesses don't think about export markets, let alone building parallel businesses abroad, when they are quite so tiny!

George's motto used to be that the turtle only got ahead by sticking its neck out, and so as a reminder, he had a rather large collection of turtles. (Mercifully, his turtles were wooden models or carved out of stone, and our house escaped the fate of being awash in a sea of turtles!) But having stuck

Sources: Adapted with permission from 1. Elsevier: Whiting, V. R., & Reardon, K. K. Strategic alliance in India: Sage Publications. In R. T. Moran, D. O. Braaten, & J. E. Walsh Jr. (Eds.), *International Business Case Studies for the Multicultural Marketplace* (pp. 58–62). Houston, TX: Gulf Publishing Company. (Copyright © 1994 by Elsevier.) 2. Jackson, Matthew, *Not Only a Grandpa* (privately published), 2002.

our necks out, we decided it was probably better to take the hit in our sales and split off the British and European territory and their sales at an early stage in our company's growth. We figured we would trade that turnover in for a chance to establish European-based publications, a European-based authorship, and an opportunity to begin the creation of a global presence.

We had been importing books selectively from a handful of British publishers for a few years starting in 1969—a program that continued into the mid-1970s. But we wanted international marketing and distribution for all our own products (books and journals). And since we strongly believed that "knowledge knows no boundaries," we also wanted to publish the best of European social science, which we figured would be easier to do from London than California. I must confess, George and I were afflicted with just a touch of wanderlust, too, so the desire to build an international publishing operation was virtually irresistible!

An Opportunity Appears

Although we enjoyed our annual trips to the UK and our relationships with executives at Allen & Unwin, Routledge, Tavistock, Faber and Faber, and Constable, there was still a great deal missing, including the lack of a real two-way trade providing marketing and distribution for SAGE books and journals in the UK.

After World War II and continuing into the 1970s, American-British publishing joint ventures typically involved American firms buying the rights to British books, and vice versa, a process that happened one book at a time. By 1971, George and I saw this process as an inefficient way to do business. We were also concerned that this method (working through the UK) would not afford us full access to the European social science market.

Our intention was to find unmet needs for high-quality, moderately priced information in the social science community. Critical to success in this niche was the acknowledgment that the producers were also consumers, where "to serve is to succeed." Another critical success factor was an ability to disseminate material quickly and to market it widely. Because buying British books one at a time would not serve the needs of SAGE, George and I looked for alternative entry points into the British and European markets.

Opening SAGE Publications, Ltd in London in mid-1971 would be a strategic move based on three premises. First, London provided a door into the European marketplace. Second, London shared English as a primary language with the United States. Finally, the sooner our move into London took place, the less we would be giving up in the transaction. Had we delayed the move to a time when foreign sales were a larger portion of SAGE, Inc.'s turnover, the task of peeling off the business to establish a joint venture would have been more difficult.

At the time we were considering the move into London, approximately 10% of our business was in the UK and continental Europe. Given SAGE, Inc.'s annual turnover of $1 million, we determined we would be handing over $100,000 of the parent company's business to another entity. As we grew, the proportion of business that would be handed over to the London venture would grow proportionately.

While we were considering the move, George and I were approached by a group of energetic and experienced book distributors who owned a company named Eurospan, Ltd. This company was set up solely for book distribution and was interested in establishing a conventional distribution contract with SAGE. We, however, were not interested in such a limited relationship.

As an alternative to a conventional book distribution contract, George and I proposed launching SAGE Publications, Ltd as a joint venture arrangement, with SAGE maintaining 60% ownership in the venture and the partners of Eurospan, Ltd acquiring the remaining 40% of the organization. Eurospan, Ltd had not previously been involved in the actual publishing of books, let alone journals. SAGE had knowledge in this area, and Eurospan had established distribution channels in the UK and quite a few in Europe, as well. The partnership would create synergy between the two companies.

In May 1971, we entered into a joint venture arrangement with the principals of Eurospan, Ltd (Peter Geelan, Peter Kershaw Taylor, and Geoff Longbottom). At that time, Eurospan was a rapidly growing distribution operation for about 10 American publishers. In the new arrangement, we would run our fledgling UK-based company out of Eurospan's facilities until such time as turnover was great enough to begin hiring staff of our own. Also, part of the plan was to start a European publishing program that would complement the existing American list and build a publishing company with its own list of books and journals. We also planned to build an aggressive international marketing capability for all SAGE products regardless of where they originated, with a strong direct-mail operation as its foundation and greatest strength.

Success and Challenges

The move into England went smoothly for a number of reasons. The economics of doing business in England were similar to business economics in the United States. No significant language barriers existed between the two countries. Trade arrangements between the United States and the United Kingdom were flexible. Similar political, legal, and religious foundations in both countries allowed both cross-cultural partners to better understand each other.

Still, the partnership was separated by an ocean, and this created challenges. While English was a common tongue, words took on different meanings on opposite sides of the ocean. When the British asked if something was "agreeable in principle" to their American partners, a "yes" was interpreted as approval to act. The Americans, however, thought they were merely communicating willingness to consider a detailed proposal. On the surface, the countries seemed alike, yet subtle communication differences caused cross-cultural challenges, as evidenced in the different interpretations of phrases such as "in principle."

A year after we had developed the joint venture agreement with Eurospan, Ltd, George and I had an opportunity to acquire five journals from the British publisher Weidenfeld and Nicholson, Ltd (the *Journal of Contemporary History* was the flagship title). The UK publishing house had decided to get out of academic journal publishing and had sold the five journals to Greenwood Press, a reprint publisher based in Connecticut (the company's name was changed to Greenwood Publishing Group, Inc. in 1990). Greenwood got the manuscripts for issues of these five journals in January 1972 and had no idea how to cope with them. All five were in danger of their current issues not being printed on time, due to a lack of manuscripts being copyedited, typeset, proofed, and printed (let alone being mailed) on schedule.

Walter Laqueur, who was at the time the senior co-editor of the *Journal of Contemporary History* and also on the editorial board of a journal I'd helped start from scratch, *Youth & Society,* was totally distraught. He called me up in a panic and asked if we would buy the journals, rescuing them from near disso-lution. The cost was ridiculously low, so we agreed, and I remember, after completing the legalities, phoning up Peter Geelan at Eurospan and saying, "Peter, you're no longer just the distributer of our books and journals; you're now in the publishing business!"

Peter knew of a bright young man, David Brooks, to head up the effort. David was running a direct-mail outlet for publishers at a collective called IBIS (International Book Information Services), a marketing company jointly owned by four major British publishing companies. Peter suggested I hire David and teach him the journal business. We were in a hurry and I had known David from my brief stint at Pergamon in Oxford, so I told Peter to hire David and put him to work as quickly as possible. David brought along a part-time secretary, and between the two of them, they got the journals caught up and published in a timely manner.

SAGE, Ltd had begun publishing in the UK, on time, on budget, and with a distinguished and satisfied network of authors and editors. David Brooks was highly organized and set up efficient computer systems to record and track our mailings, which at that time was the sole selling strategy used at SAGE, Ltd—as indeed it was at SAGE, Inc. SAGE, Ltd had a database and a customer base, as well as all its financial information, on its computer. SAGE, Inc. used its computer and outside computing services mainly for accounting functions, marketing, circulation, and distribution, not for budgeting or as a sophisticated management tool.

By the time SAGE, Ltd was founded in 1971, the American branch, with its five-year start, was already well established in the United States and had the advantage of being an American company selling into its home market. Because SAGE, Ltd was selling American products in the UK and Europe, it was perceived initially as an American company. A SAGE, Inc. product was unmistakably American in spelling and punctuation and, in many instances, in authorship. SAGE, Ltd, therefore, started life with a product that in the main was not widely acceptable to its new market.

SAGE, Ltd's turnover in 1971 was about 30,000 pounds sterling, and the profit was nil. In fact, if George and I had not seen SAGE, Ltd as a long-term investment and had not agreed to extended payment terms for its prod-uct as part of SAGE, Ltd's capitalization, there would have been a very con-siderable loss.

An Important Link: Matthew Jackson

Later that year, as the staff expanded, George and I invited Matthew Jackson into SAGE, Ltd as a consultant. From George's point of view, Matt was to ensure that the management worked hard and long, selling and delivering SAGE, Inc. products with the greatest possible economy. My requirement of Matt was slightly different. Because Matt had lived and worked in the United States and had lost what was perceived as British stiffness and reserve, and the air of superiority so disliked by Americans, I thought he could also serve as a key communication link, explaining and interpreting each side to the other.

I had first met Matt in 1963 when I was working in England as a Book Sales Manager at Pergamon Press in Oxford. Matt was lecturing at a sales management course in London that I was attending in order to determine if my UK salesmen should be enrolled. Lecturers were required to eat lunch with the course members, and so Matt made a point of sitting next to me, having noticed that I was American and also the only woman in the course.

In his privately published 2002 memoir, *Not Only a Grandpa,* Matt describes how he became involved in our lives and in SAGE.

Not Only a Grandpa
Matthew Jackson

Sara was a pretty 23-year-old, and at lunch we got on well together. She was rather startled when I invited her home for the weekend following the end of the course. Paul and David were respectively 7 and 5, and Sara was reassured to learn that I lived at home with my wife and two sons. Marian and Sara took to each other and Sara was obviously very fond of the boys. We agreed to keep in touch, and shortly afterwards Sara phoned to say that she had left Pergamon and was returning to her home town New York.

. . . [I]n 1965 Sara phoned to say she'd formed a publishing company called SAGE Inc. with George McCune, and in 1967, she called to say she'd married George and they were coming to England as part of their honeymoon.

When they arrived in London, I collected them at the station so they could spend time with me and my family. I can still see George, as he and Sara came out of the station, a big, burly man. As Sara introduced us, he spoke slowly and quietly and smiled as Sara and I kissed. I knew that George and I would be friends, which we were until he died. We argued, disagreed, walked in companionable silence in London and California, and after not meeting perhaps for months, always picked up our friendship when next we met, as though there had never been a gap.

George was a master publisher with comprehensive knowledge of the publishing industry. Most of what I know after 30 years' working in publishing stems from my discussions with George. He verbalized many basic truths about running a publishing company, and part of my work with SAGE in London was to hold on to his and Sara's vision of the company and bring us back to those first principles if we deviated.

Matt's consultancy fee that first year was based on a rate of £30 a day, but we could not afford to pay him, so he graciously waived his fees. The following year, our situation was much the same. Turnover had risen slightly, but we had not developed the mass of volume of product needed for profit.

Sailing Ahead

By January 1972, David Brooks had become Managing Director of SAGE, Ltd, which was located in Hatton Garden in London's diamond district. The company had only six or seven employees at this time, including David and Katy, the woman who had become his wife.

The previous summer, Katy, who had been George's secretary, went over to England with a letter of recommendation to begin working at SAGE London. She soon fell in love with David and they got married, producing a lovely boy named Nicholas. They also had a temperamental Irish setter whose coat was roughly the color of Katy's hair, which was red as befitting her Irish heritage.

The Brooks family lived in Hampstead, and over the years Katy became an editor at SAGE, Ltd, working with Walter Laqueur and taking the manuscripts of his journal to be copyedited, proofread, and printed. David handled the marketing and business end of the company. Eventually, the couple divorced, and Katy returned to the United States, where she lived with their son in Connecticut.

In 1973, an interesting event developed that would demonstrate Matt Jackson's loyalty to us and our company. Eurospan decided to withdraw its investment from SAGE and offered back its shareholding. Matt told George he would be glad to accept the shares in lieu of payment. George was taken aback at what he saw as a very generous offer on Matt's part, and warned him, "Matt, you will be tying up your money with no chance of it producing a return, because SAGE is a private company and always will be. It will never declare a dividend. All profits will go back to develop the company."

Matt understood but still wanted to go ahead, and soon became the holder of 50 apparently forever worthless shares. In 1973, we invited Matt to join SAGE, Ltd's Board as a nonexecutive director, and he immediately agreed. For almost 37 years, Matt has been associated with SAGE, and I feel he is very much part of our company and family.

During that period, I remember George and I were returning from a trip to Morocco and stopped in London to meet with Walter Laqueur, Jeremiah (Jerry) Kaplan (who George knew well from Macmillan and who had founded the Free Press), and David Brooks and his wife. Walter had co-founded the *Journal of Contemporary History* with George Mosse to publish historical articles about the Nazi regime, although the journal also spanned European history from World War I up to the war in Vietnam.

We had brought back gifts of book covers made out of hand-sewn leather with attached markers to hold one's place, sized for small paperback volumes. Since there wasn't any holiday gift wrapping paper available to me in Marrakech, I wrapped each gift in pages from an Arabic newspaper. Walter, who was fluent in Arabic as well as German, and also Jewish, started reading from his copy of the Arabic newspaper, and as he did, he became more and more intent. Finally, he let us all know that what he was reading was that the Arabic newspapers were basically proclaiming death to all Jews!

I don't read Arabic, so had no idea I had given both Walter and Jerry, who was also Jewish, a gift with such highly offensive gift wrap. But being Jewish myself, I thought I could be somewhat excused for my ignorance of the Arabic language. George, however, was mortified. He'd been a Sunday school teacher, and not only was smart and well educated (thanks to the G.I. Bill) but also had a highly developed sense of ethics and a strong set of values, especially about how we should treat our fellow human beings.

Walter, who was a UK citizen, subsequently became an honorary citizen of the United States, Israel, and France. For SAGE's 40th Anniversary celebration, he provided the following testimonial about SAGE:

A Celebration in Words: SAGE 1965–2005

Walter Laqueur, *Professor, Co-founder, Journal of Contemporary History*

SAGE and the *Journal of Contemporary History* are contemporaries, born the same year—1965. I met Sara and George at 4 Devonshire Street, London—I believe it was a sunny day and they were staying in a hotel near Marble Arch—and we quickly reached agreement. Little did we know then that from the small beginning a little empire (SAGE) would develop, and that our journal would not only last 40+ years but become a leader in its field. There is little to report about the years between—no turbulence, no crisis—and cooperation could not have been smoother.

End of the First Decade

The year 1976 marked our 10th year in business, and we celebrated by throwing modest but well-attended 10th anniversary parties at the major academic meetings in 1975–1976.

All of our networking activity over the previous decade was starting to pay off. Our imprint was gaining luster. SAGE Publications, Ltd was established in London not only as a strong distributor but also as a small but growing and caring originator of innovative work by UK and European authors. The cross-pollination between social scientists in North America and Western Europe was growing by leaps and bounds—and so, too, were enrollments in social science courses in these regions.

The number of authors and scholarly societies we published and had under contract was also growing. It was a struggle to find the money to do all that we wanted to do. Our journals list was the foundation, underpinning both the networking and the financing of our growth on both sides of the Atlantic Ocean.

The faith and support of our authors, who were our advisers, opening successive doors for us, was truly overwhelming. People like Donald Campbell, James S. Coleman, Morris Janowitz, F. Gerald (Jerry) Kline, Marilyn Gittell, Beverly Duncan, and Jessie Bernard (to name but a few of the dozens of hardworking and brilliant academic editors and editorial advisers that we had during those years) truly put us on the map (see more about this development in Chapter 6). They and their colleagues and star students helped us over and over to expand that map in both the breadth and depth of our offerings—with quality, value for the money, and speedy publication dates as advantages we offered in return. Our royalties were fair but not above the norm (and, in times of recession, occasionally late). Our covers were honest as to content and author(s), but not colorful. Our marketing (if I do say so myself) was extraordinary. We worked long and hard to reach the niches where our offerings could be utilized—and they were.

We tried to provide publications and services that our authors and their students told us were needed, succeeding in our response more often than not. We helped scholars and students to communicate with their peers and with policy makers who were interested in or open to innovative solutions to social problems and issues. This ability to keep our ear close to the ground of the scholarly community provided us with the opportunity to build a program that is considered the jewel in our crown, that of research methods, statistics, and evaluation.

CHAPTER 5

Shaping Research Methods

As we were growing, we realized that having an emphasis on research methods was something that was common across many disciplines, something that was of interest to many different authors across a variety of fields, and by providing that, we differentiated ourselves.

Because we firmly believed in publishing material from fields that were in and of themselves interdisciplinary, many of our research methods could be transferred from politics to sociology, economics, or studies of health, as well as to topics of interest to government policy makers (delinquency, risk-taking behavior, allocation of scarce monetary resources, and so on). As we did our sales analysis, it became very obvious that there was a definite advantage to looking at broadening our publishing on research methods.

That conclusion was, in addition, validated by some of the early journal publishing that we did, after testing out topics in the *American Behavioral Scientist*. In that way, we found out that research methods in communication attracted great interest, and they provided new and challenging ways to study the mass media and find out more about how things tick. The same was true in many fields in the social and behavioral sciences, including interdisciplinary areas such as criminology, family studies, urban studies, and so on.

As I have said, our competitive advantage in those early days—and this has, I think, continued to be true—was that we were widely regarded as being very friendly to interdisciplinary research. In contrast to this most publishers in those

Source: John W. Creswell from his 2009 SAGE published report, *How SAGE Has Shaped Research Methods: A 40-Year History*.

days (and I think, to some extent, even more recently) tended to have a "silo" effect in their editorial and marketing programs—having specialists in sociology, specialists in political science, specialists in economics, in psychology— while we went across those fields as much as we could.

Within less than a decade, we found ourselves becoming the "natural home" for work in research methods—for example, the "little green books," the *Quantitative Applications in the Social Sciences* (*QASS*), which were the first of our *University Paper* series, and quickly became best sellers.

It had begun with our *QASS* series, the "little green books" that were so successful (see Chapter 3, p. 22) with scholars in the social sciences. From there we continued to expand, growing in both quantitative and qualitative research methodology, evaluation, general research methods and techniques, and mixed methods. The story of how SAGE grew to shape the field of research methodology is the subject of this chapter.

Evaluation: The Chicken or the Egg?

If SAGE provided encouragement for quantitative methods by publishing the *QASS* series, it had an even more substantive role in the development of the field of evaluation and evaluation methods. Considering the emerging field back in the 1970s, we wondered whether the field of evaluation built SAGE, or SAGE built the field of evaluation—a classic example of the chicken-or-the-egg question.

SAGE's early involvement with the field of evaluation began in 1974 when we successfully competed to publish the *Handbook of Evaluation Research* (Struening & Guttentag, 1975). It was actually the first time I had ever heard the word *evaluation,* and it was spoken by a lady who subsequently became a very dear person in my life, Marcia Guttentag. At the time we were preparing to publish the two-volume set of the *Handbook* in 1975, we knew we were gambling heavily—"betting the store," if it didn't work, especially since publication came on the heels of a major recession.

In 1974, we experienced the culmination of what I would call Mr. Nixon's recession, a couple of years in which we went through a rather bad patch. In addition, in the summer of 1974, George had a heart attack and was out of commission for a year in terms of working at his former pace. The combination of events had us come fairly close to bankruptcy, but we recovered and strengthened our publishing program. We grew the company and achieved our first million-dollar year in sales, and then subsequently passed many other years where sales climbed into multiple millions.

For a ten-year-old fledgling social science publishing house, however, publication of such a large-scale project as the *Handbook* was a bold venture. Up until the 1970s, evaluation was largely unknown to publishers and academics. There were no mailing lists, for example, that were commercially available to rent. Finding the market for evaluation literature clearly was going to be the key to the success of our gamble.

Knowing we'd be in serious trouble if our plan didn't work, we decided to take the risk and began publication. I remember the reaction of a distinguished sociologist who visited our office during the summer while the *Handbook* was in production. "How many of these are you going to print?" he asked me. When I told him 3,000, he replied, "If I were you, I'd only print 2,000. You'll have a hard time selling those."

But contrary to what the conventional wisdom would have us believe, the response to the publication of the *Handbook of Evaluation Research* was enormous from all disciplines. And it was swift. We printed 3,000 copies as we had initially planned, but we cautiously ordered the printer to bind only half of them. When the truck arrived, the orders in response to our first direct mail drop were coming in so fast and furiously, we had to phone the binder and tell him to bind the rest as fast as he could. When those arrived, less than a month later, we were already asking the printer and bindery how soon they could produce and deliver more.

It was 1975, and our experience with the *Handbook* taught us there was an important need here—a special and unusual need that had not been met. Academics were hungry for evaluation tools. Evaluation was being added to every grant, and individuals needed to cite the tools of evaluation they were using. Mitch Allen, our editor for sociology and other disciplines, who did much to increase our methodology list in the field of qualitative analysis, later described our decision to publish evaluation texts as "insightful and enlightened."

Eager to fill the perceived gap, we began our networking process on a high-priority basis, which led us to Gene Glass, among others, to start the *Evaluation Studies Review Annual* series. At the same time, we started searching for an editor for our first journal in evaluation, *Evaluation Quarterly,* now the bimonthly *Evaluation Review.* Howard Freeman nobly volunteered his time and effort for that cause and enlisted Peter Rossi to advise and help. Both Howie and Pete were incredible to work with—insightful, responsive, and alike in their insistence on clear, concise writing. What a gift to a publisher!

In 1977, at the national meeting of the American Sociological Association in Chicago, I met Michael Quinn Patton. We were actively looking for manuscripts to fill gaps in the evaluation literature, not only to grow our company but to grow the emerging field as well. Michael was attending the meeting, hoping to attract a publisher for a manuscript he was writing, later to become *Utilization-Focused Evaluation.* He dropped off a copy of his prospectus at the SAGE booth, and I immediately recognized it as pointing to an important new book. Within a half hour, I called Michael at his hotel room requesting to see more. After reading the five chapters he had drafted, I saw the market potential of his work and invited him to have dinner with George and me that very evening.

We didn't enter into an agreement that evening, but we did offer to have Michael's chapters reviewed by Marv Alkin, whose work in utilization has been enormously important to the field. Meanwhile, Michael kept his options open, only to find that none of the other publishers he dealt with seemed to fully understand the book or its place in the literature, nor could any of them describe how they would market the book. Recounting the story years later, he told me that what impressed him about SAGE was that even though he was a young and inexperienced author, we treated him as if it was a privilege for us to publish his manuscript.

Well, we thought it was, and we turned out to be absolutely right in that regard! Indeed, *Utilization* became an instant best seller and today is in its fourth edition. Subsequently, I enjoyed many conversations with Michael and encouraged him to write *Qualitative Evaluation Methods*—another book we recognized would fill a gap in the field—offering him and his family the use of our cabin in Yosemite as a retreat, should he need a writer's getaway.

Along the way, we discovered that evaluation, even more than other inter-disciplinary fields in which we had been publishing during the first decade of our company's existence, moved us from a strictly academic publishing market into the government market. This meant our entry into a market of very special practitioners: the users, producers, and consumers of applied social research. In a way, that move was an eye-opener for us and taught us many valuable lessons.

Many more successes in publishing evaluation materials followed. The following year (1978), SAGE published *Evaluation: A Systematic Approach* (Rossi and Freeman), which used an experimental approach to examine large programs. *Evaluation* is now it its seventh edition (Rossi, Lipsey, and Freeman). Another success, the *Program Evaluation Kit* (Morris, 1978), was developed at UCLA's Center for the Study of Evaluation, and signed with us in part because we were the only publisher who agreed to do it as eight paperback volumes rather than as one massive book. Again, the *Program Evaluation Kit* was a gamble, but the gamble paid off. A decade later, with the second edition just out, we had sold over $2 million worth of the *Kit* to professionals in the field.

In 1988, SAGE's preeminence in evaluation methods drew the attention of the American Evaluation Association (AEA). In recognition of SAGE's contribution to the field, which had seen a phenomenal spurt of growth fueled by funding from government grants, they honored me with the Association's *Lifetime Contribution Award*. Evaluation as a field had become institutionalized in so many ways in less then 15 years, and already, a new generation had been trained to join the pioneers.

In receiving the AEA award, I experienced the full-circle honor of being introduced by Michael Quinn Patton, who, 10 years after we published *Utilization-Focused Evaluation,* had become the Association's president. But in my acceptance speech, I was clear that the credit did not go to me alone or even to George and me, but also to our many hardworking staffers, as well as the top-flight scholars on whom we had depended over the years to build and develop our lists in the field of evaluation and applied social research.

As active participants, these people responded to our requests to work (and work hard!) on a particular project, or they shared insights and advice with us that educated us profoundly. They became friends as well as colleagues as we sought their help and were extremely generous in sharing their energy, knowledge, and wisdom. To this day, I am enormously grateful for the contributions of all those involved in our evaluation publishing ventures, not just to me as a professional publisher and businesswoman but to me as an individual. This is true of so many of the fields in which we developed our publishing programs, and I know other editors at SAGE Publications (both in the United States and abroad) have had the same sort of experience. It is really hard to succeed (let alone aim to excel) in the publishing business without the cooperation and dedication of one's authors.

In the 1990s and into the new millennium, SAGE has continued to be a leader in evaluation publishing. The SAGE Research Methods "Classics" Catalog of 2009 shows how evaluation unfolded in the years after the 1970s, especially during the 1990s and up to the present. Specialized books emerged as evaluation came into its own as a field of study, a path undoubtedly aided by SAGE's strong relationships with the leading authors, editors, and societies in this area.

A quick perusal of *Foundations of Program Evaluation*—a "classic" by William R. Shadish, Thomas D. Cook, and Laura C. Leviton, published in 1991—detailed the roots and theories of evaluation through the works of social science and education luminaries such as Michael Scriven, Donald Campbell, Lee Cronbach, Peter Rossi, Robert Stake, and others. Books were published by SAGE on program evaluation, collaboration and empower-ment, real-world policy, and the introduction to and the practice of evalua-tion. Not surprisingly, Stephanie Adams, current Marketing Manager for research methods at SAGE who developed the idea of the "classics" catalog, cites evaluation as a major trend in the future of SAGE's publishing.

An answer to the question of the chicken-or-the-egg phenomenon— whether SAGE as a publishing house helped to build the field of evaluation or whether evaluation as a field helped to build SAGE—is now clear. The truth is that both statements are correct at one and the same time!

Shaping Qualitative Research Methods

In the 1970s, qualitative methods were just beginning to develop. SAGE pub-lished works by a number of sociologists who studied deviance and every-day life on the urban fringe. Many had been influenced by Erving Goffman and other symbolic interaction pioneers. Our first truly qualitative methods book, Jack Douglas's *Investigative Social Research,* was published in 1976, and from there, slowly but surely, the qualitative methods list continued to expand.

Scott A. Greer, a well-known sociologist who made many contributions to urban studies, was also a forerunner to the qualitative movement (and sadly, died young—I believe he was only in his late 50s). He was very influential, introducing us to some of the key players (and their successful students) who were laying the foundations of the new qualitative research techniques and methods in sociology, including a lot of influential authors that the Free Press had published in the late 1950s and early 1960s. Another adviser was Anselm Strauss, who turned out a core group of graduate students to start a journal that we originally called *Urban Life & Culture* (when we changed the title to the *Journal of Contemporary Ethnography,* it really took off). In the early 1970s, those students were the "young Turks" and the leaders of the pack when it came to qualitative methods.

In those days, anthropology and sociology departments on college campuses were next door to each other or in the same building, often a minority, while the quantitative people—the "quantoids," as they were sometimes called—were more dominant in the social (and physical) sciences. As a result, the people who were interested in qualitative methods tended to stick together regardless of what their discipline was.

Anthropologists had been using qualitative methods since Margaret Mead's day (and before), but it was a relatively new approach for other newer subfields of sociology. Qualitative approaches never relied on the statistical methods that were especially useful in managing and analyzing large amounts of data. People today don't necessarily remember the division that existed between people who favored quantitative over qualitative techniques (and vice versa). So many people in the 1960s and 1970s believed it was robust science to crunch numbers and not robust science if you were doing fieldwork, interviews, or case studies to arrive at your results. Real wars were waged in this schism, some that came to actual fisticuffs. But whether qualitative or quantitative, the issue came down to being able to replicate findings and how well the results could be aggregated, whether the methodology was using words or numbers.

Thinking back, I'm amazed that we actually got away with publishing people from both camps. In most instances during those decades, we had good relationships with people who ideologically (in their disciplines or their fields or subfields) were basically at odds. On the other hand, at least there was some respect for opposing views, which isn't always the case when academics or politicians come together. Respect for opposing views seems to come in cycles—look at the Republicans versus the Democrats today. Viewed over time, it's clear there's been a lot of switching back and forth between the two.

David M. Fetterman, an early author we published in qualitative research and currently at Stanford University School of Medicine, gives a peek into what was going on in that area, from his testimonial in *A Celebration in Words:*

A Celebration in Words: SAGE 1965–2005
David M. Fetterman, *Stanford University School of Medicine*

SAGE was one of the first publishers to understand and publish ethnographic or qualitative research and textbooks. My early books, in 1984, *Ethnography in Educational Evaluation* and, in 1986, *Educational Evaluation: Ethnography in Theory, Practice, and Politics* are testament to their insight and understanding. This is no small feat, as qualitative research and evaluation was still in a pariah status in educational research and evaluation, in comparison to quantitative research and evaluation at the time.

By the time SAGE published my book *Ethnography: Step by Step* (1989), qualitative research had become the norm. This was in large part a function of SAGE's commitment to publishing earlier qualitative work. This helped convince our colleagues of the merits of qualitative research. Once again, this was possible only because SAGE took the risk and understood the discipline enough to venture out and take some calculated risks. *Ethnography: Step by Step* reached its 13th printing by the time a second edition was requested. Once again, SAGE's investment in publishing in qualitative research early on paid off.

In 1980, Michael Quinn Patton's *Qualitative Evaluation Methods* bridged the research worlds of evaluation, namely the quantitative methodologies (suitable for enormous data sets), which had previously dominated the field, and qualitative methods.

Knowing that research was a feature of all the social sciences and many related professional fields, we reasoned that these tools for doing research could be sold alongside other books that we published. Marketing plans were retooled, a "methods" page (or two) was added to every discipline cata-log, and the hunt for books to fill that page intensified. We began to use regu-lar direct mailing on research methods, and editors assigned to different discipline areas all searched for good methods texts. The size of the qualita-tive catalog today is a clear indication of how much this area has grown.

Just as we had done for quantitative methods, we capitalized on the inter-est in qualitative methods by launching a series, this one entitled the *Qualitative Research Methods (QRM)* series. Our marketing strategy was to transfer one good idea to another area. The editorial team was made up of dynamic social scientists from a broad range of disciplines: John Van Maanen from management, Peter K. Manning from criminology, and Marc L. Miller from applied anthropology. Authors also came from multiple disciplines and from both sides of the Atlantic Ocean.

With standard dark blue covers, the books in the *QRM* series were simi-lar to the *QASS* titles in size, look, and utility, but they were less technique oriented. Michael Agar authored a book on ethnography (*Speaking of Ethnography,* 1986), Nigel G. Fielding penned one on linking data (*Linking Data,* 1986), and Jerome Kirk and Marc L. Miller wrote on reliability and validity (*Reliability and Validity in Qualitative Research,* 1986). Today, there are 52 volumes in this series, sometimes known in-house as the "little blue books."

New Ways of Thinking About Research Methods

In the early 1980s, the way for us to bridge new ideas in research methods was often to copycat old ideas. Writing about reliability and validity from a qualitative spin advanced a new method within already accepted parameters. But when readers looked inside the book, they saw something different. As an example, authors Matthew B. Miles and Michael Huberman addressed familiar data analysis steps in research but from a qualitative context. Soon after, a book by Yvonna S. Lincoln and Egon G. Guba on naturalistic inquiry provided insight into familiar case study research but highlighted the axiom-atic philosophical differences between postpositive and naturalistic inquiry.

As early as 1988, SAGE London published a book on human inquiry by Peter W. Reason, titled *Human Inquiry in Action,* and in 1989 brought out Jaber F. Gubrium and David Silverman's book, *The Politics of Field Research.* Whether consciously or subconsciously, the authors of these books eased many researchers into a new way of thinking about research methods.

During the 1990s, SAGE published specialized, procedural qualitative books on techniques, such as grounded theory, heuristic and phenomenological methods, social research, ethnography, case study research, the practice of qualitative research, and, in 1998, Uwe Flick's *An Introduction to Qualitative Research.* The diversity of these approaches certainly got the attention of the research community. In 1998, SAGE published John W. Creswell's qualitative methods book that compared five methods for conducting qualitative inquiry.

In 1994, SAGE published a book that was to shape the meaning of qualitative research for many people worldwide: Norman K. Denzin and Yvonna S. Lincoln's *Handbook of Qualitative Research.* Denzin wrote in a private note that this book was the "lynch-pin in SAGE's entire qualitative methodology publishing program."

It is this indeed, and back in 1994, the title solidified our role in the landscape of qualitative inquiry. Even more important, the *Handbook* curiously reshaped the field with each new edition, first with the interpretive approach, second a postmodern emphasis, and third a social justice orientation. Qualitative writers responded accordingly. With the trend toward pedagogy and smaller, more useful books, the Denzin and Lincoln *Handbook* is also available in three smaller books, presenting an ideal package for classroom use. We have done this with other handbooks, where appropriate.

The journal *Qualitative Inquiry,* edited by Norman K. Denzin, was launched in 1995 and became a natural home for the discussions around these new ways of thinking, exploring the qualitative framework within a multidisciplinary approach. The growth of this journal over 16 years stands as further evidence of the rapid expansion of this field.

As well as expanding our book publishing program in qualitative methods, we ventured into qualitative software products during the 1990s. In 1995, SAGE created Scolari, a software division to market several qualitative data analysis products, such as NUD*IST (later to evolve into NVivo), SAGE/SRM Database of Social Research Methodology on CD-ROM,

Diction (a text analysis program), and Decision Explorer (an idea mapping and strategy tool). These were joined by other qualitative data analysis software products, such as Atlas.ti, WinMax (later MAXqda), the Ethnograph, HyperRESEARCH, and Code-a-Text. Other additions included the survey software programs SphinxSurvey and Results for Research, the research design program of Methodologists Toolchest, and the BEST program for the observation and analysis of behavior. By 2004, we had discontinued these software sales due to Internet availability and other changes in the marketplace, but for a number of years, they represented yet another type of research methods "product" for SAGE.

The diversity in the qualitative product line was matched by the diversity in disciplinary affiliation of our authors: from education and sociology to anthropology and nursing. This diversity continues today with recent books espousing the "interpretive turn" of qualitative inquiry that the Denzin and Lincoln handbooks heralded. SAGE has published books on postmodern interviewing, critical theory, empowerment, action research, feminist research, family studies, communication, and psychology. Like children leaving home, the fragmentation of qualitative methods from overviews to discipline-specific books has showed both a breaking away and remaining within the family of qualitative methods. Throughout the development of qualitative research, SAGE has helped to stimulate and enhance an even broader interest in research methods.

General Research Methods and Techniques

Research techniques really took form at SAGE during the 1980s and 1990s, although they had always been important to us (and our authors). A centerpiece of this entire area was the launch of another small book series in 1984, the *Applied Social Research Methods* (*ASRM*) series, edited by Leonard Bickman. This now 51-volume series started with Floyd J. Fowler's book on survey research in 1984 and continued with a classic on literature reviews by Harris Cooper, case study research by Robert K. Yin, and biography by Norman K. Denzin in 1989. These short, practical books touched on many applied topics, including ethics, design, meta-analysis, scale development, randomized experiments, and ethnography. It is important to note that these books spanned the areas of quantitative and qualitative methods.

C. Deborah Laughton, an acquisitions editor at SAGE for more than a decade, attributes the success of these books to their status as pedagogy books that could be used in the classroom. To be published under this category, a book had to pass the "flip test," meaning the books needed to be useful and practical for readers as they "flipped" through them. The *Applied Social Research Methods* series met this test.

Other general methods and technique books we published include Delbert C. Miller's *Handbook of Research Design and Social Measurement* in 1991 and the applied *Survey Kit* in 2000, edited by Arlene Fink at UCLA. (Arlene, one of the key movers behind the *Survey Kit,* a research methods best seller, authored one of our best-selling texts in survey research before we had formally begun our full-court press textbook publishing program in the 1990s.)

"How-to" books for graduate students were also developed, on such topics as developing proposals and surviving the dissertation. A survival skills series commissioned in the early 1990s ran to some 17 titles, including *Getting Your Book Published* and *Successful Publishing in Scholarly Journals.* John W. Creswell's *Research Design* on designing dissertation proposals, came out in 1994. Because it bridged quantitative and qualitative research, *Research Design* foreshadowed the mixed methods approach.

We also developed encyclopedias on research methods, including social research (Michael Lewis-Beck, Alan E. Bryman, and Tim Futing Liao, *The SAGE Encyclopedia of Social Science Research Methods,* 2004), evaluation, survey research, qualitative methods, and case study research. Handbooks showcased research methods through state-of-the-art chapters written by leading authorities in the field: on interviewing, action research, ethics, and mixed methods. Dictionaries, such as W. Paul Vogt's *Dictionary of Statistics and Methodology* (3rd edition published May 2005) and Thomas A. Schwandt's *Dictionary of Qualitative Inquiry,* also helped to provide simple definitions and explanations of concepts to guide scholars thorough their own investigations.

Mixed Methods

The idea of mixed methods was one that grew at SAGE over a number of years. In 1988, a book of what was called "multimethod research" was written by two sociologists, John Brewer and Albert Hunter. Around the same time, John W. Creswell was writing *Research Design,* in which he not only referenced the evaluation writers but also advanced one entire chapter devoted to combining research approaches. SAGE soon published Abbas Tashakkori and Charles Teddlie's *Handbook of Mixed Methods.* This handbook solidified SAGE's efforts in mixed methods through its encouragement of the formation of a worldwide community that believed that quantitative and qualitative research should speak to one another. This led to mixed methods being incorporated into several of SAGE's general methods books written for disciplinary audiences, including these areas: media and communication, education and psychology, social work, social research, and family research.

With this new focus, a journal devoted to mixed methods seemed logical. John W. Creswell tells how he was instrumental in bringing about the *Journal of Mixed Methods Research:*

> In 2005, my colleague Abbas Tashakkori and I had lunch with Blaise Simqu, President and CEO of SAGE, to talk about the possibility of [a journal on mixed methods]. Blaise listened to our pitch intently and then asked an important question: "Does mixed methods provide a better understanding of a research question than either quantitative or qualitative research alone?" It was a great question and one that I continue to field from workshop audiences. Although writers of mixed methods studies provide anecdotal evidence that answers this question, I still work on ideas for confirmation.
>
> Nevertheless, the luncheon conversation must have been successful, for in 2007, SAGE agreed to launch the *Journal of Mixed Methods Research* with a highly-distinguished editorial board bringing together the premier researchers and practitioners working in the field. The journal has helped to legitimize the field of mixed methods, providing researchers with a common language and shared forum to express their approach, regardless of geographic or subject boundaries.

Soon after, other books on mixed methods followed. In 2007, *Designing and Conducting Mixed Methods Research* (John W. Creswell and Vicki L. Plano Clark) was published, followed in 2008 by a book edited by the same authors, *The Mixed Methods Reader,* which provided examples of published mixed methods studies and discussions. In 2006, SAGE London issued a four-volume set on mixed methods edited by Alan Bryman and another edited book on advances in mixed methods in 2008 by Manfred Max Bergman. In the United States, in 2009, we published Teddlie and Tashakkori's *Foundations of Mixed Methods Research* exploring and extending their views from their 1998 mixed methodology book. With the growing popularity of mixed methods, we can now look back and see how SAGE helped and supported the development of this newly emergent research technique.

SAGE's Past and Future in Research Methods

Today, as publisher of more than 60 new research methods titles a year (a significant percentage of our current annual average of published books), SAGE is the largest research methods publisher in the world. This does not include the total of articles on research methodology disseminated annually by our journals division. In retrospect, SAGE's commitment to research methods has been evident through the years in a number of ways:

• SAGE has supported, encouraged, and perhaps even helped in the discovery of multiple research fields: evaluation, qualitative research, and mixed methods. Scholars may have invented methods, but SAGE had a hand in shaping the growing market.

• SAGE packaged research methods in a way that made them accessible, concise, timely, affordable, and practical for pedagogical use. These books found classroom use as pedagogical tools at a time when research methods were often considered a difficult subject for students.

• The SAGE methods publications were peer-reviewed, which ensured the highest quality. Editors of the various SAGE series compiled lists of the books needed in the field and sought out authors who were experts.

• SAGE developed and marketed its methods content across disciplines. Editors asked authors to include examples in their books from a variety of disciplines, and SAGE added a methods page to each discipline-focused catalog. All SAGE acquisitions editors (in the United States, the UK, and India) were encouraged to acquire methods books in their various disciplines; thus authors came from many discipline fields, providing differing viewpoints about epistemology and about techniques. Such diversity is a hallmark of research methods as a field.

- SAGE provided a diverse product line through handbooks, series, encyclopedias, kits, stand-alone books, and journals, which meant that these products found many applications as classroom texts, reference works, aids for professionals, guides for evaluators, and materials for workshop consultants. Ideas that worked well with one type of product were often used to initiate another product.

- SAGE had breakthroughs in research methods that were unanticipated. The "little green books" (QASS) immediately grew in popularity, the evaluation field was propelled by assessment needs from funding agencies, talented acquisition editors landed authors who were great content specialists, a classics catalog was developed to keep popular titles in front of audiences, and direct mail marketing and, more recently, electronic communication, including e-mail and social media outreach, helped to reach academics directly and closely track what books and journals they needed in which fields.

- SAGE encouraged, signed, and reached out to authors who came from many disciplines and were often master writers who developed close relationships with acquisition editors. As Vicki Knight, Senior Research Methods Acquisition Editor has said, "SAGE is not so big that people in the company do not know who the authors are."

SAGE also helped to support the development of many research methods communities. Long-standing publishing partnerships exist with some of the world's leading research societies, including the American Evaluation Association and the Tavistock Institute. International events such as the Mixed Methods Conference in the UK and the International Congress of Qualitative Inquiry, headed up by Norman Denzin, have grown and been legitimized with SAGE's support. The partnerships extend across many disciplines too. Research methods have, in effect, opened many doors for SAGE into new areas of publishing, such as psychology, nursing, and health.

SAGE continues to support new researchers too, with initiatives like the SAGE/BERA Research into Practice awards and sponsorship of the Times

Higher Awards Research Project of the Year in 2008, offering opportunities to profile and reward important new research.

New Trends in Research Methods

Today, acquisitions editors, including Patrick Brindle and Vicki Knight, help to continue the drive in publishing the latest trends in research methods, including online interviewing, video and audio data collection procedures, and technology and its use in data collection. There is also a renewed interest in evaluation, increased interest in qualitative research in the health sciences, a focus on narrative research, a greater sensitivity to ethical issues, research training, the systematic syntheses of literature and data, and an emphasis on social justice research.

SAGE is also exploring opportunities in online research methods and creating new value for SAGE products. In March 2009, SAGE initiated MethodSpace, a social network created for those working in or with an interest in research methods. SAGE is also developing a new online research tool that will pull together research methods content in a way that enables users to access and manipulate the sources for their research needs. (See Chapter 11, p. 140, for more on MethodSpace and the new online research tool.)

Looking ahead, the question is not *if* SAGE will shape new research methods in the future but *how* it will. Based on the past, individuals working from many discipline perspectives will develop research methods, crafting them for use by a broad range of audiences. Research methods constitute a common denominator for many scholars, the thread that binds them together, regardless of field, demographics, or country of origin. As we have seen in the past, new research methods will take shape, and, I am confident, will be supported and encouraged, once again, by SAGE.

CHAPTER 6

SAGE's Legacy in Social and Behavioral Sciences

A large part of SAGE's legacy is in publishing newly emerging fields in the social and behavioral sciences in the 1960s and those that sprouted or began rapidly growing into the 1970s and 1980s. The background of how SAGE shaped the social sciences through scholarly publishing (and was shaped in return by many wonderful social scientists) begins with the story of George's and my earlier careers and the association we had with a remarkable man, Jeremiah (Jerry) Kaplan. That story was told in Chapter 1; in this chapter, I will attempt to reconstruct the events and connections that followed, altering the course of SAGE, as well as to some degree the course of social and behavioral sciences in the world.

From Branches to Twigs

The era right after World War II was a time when social scientists still believed in writing in accessible English (as opposed to later, when they wrote mostly in jargon, and in footnotes, that only a few could understand, perhaps if they were in the same subfield). In that period, sociology was still a more coherent discipline, and people were writing for a broad or more general readership. That was also true of political science and psychology. Researchers still had to have a foundation in the Greats, whether it was in translation like

Weber or Durkheim, or whether it was the seminal works of the incredible social scientists who were at universities like Harvard, Chicago, Yale, Berkeley, or Stanford.

Many of these early Greats were refugees from Nazi Germany, and often they had come to England or the United States in the late 1930s or just after World War II to do their college and graduate work here. Or they were second generations who might have been the first persons in their family to go to college and graduate or get a Ph.D. These were the people who were the most formative and inspiring in discipline after discipline, field after field.

Seymour Martin (Marty) Lipset from New York City, a Free Press author, was a good friend and one of the great post–World War II sociologists. Marty's area was political sociology, and he was an adviser to us when we first knew him at Stanford. He wrote at least one book chapter for us that I remember as being an incredible opportunity to see what it was like to do wonderful sociology and bring terrific graduate students into the field in the post–World War II era.

In the 1970s, there was a noticeable change, as academics and publishers were talking about the "twigging" going on in discipline after discipline. It was no longer just physics, but *nuclear* physics or *bio*physics, or *aero*physics. The same kind of division was happening in the field of sociology. The main tree was developing new branches, and those branches were twigging, in both the literature being produced and the ability of sociologists to communicate with one another. Networks within sociology were forming that focused on subfields, such as family studies, criminology, mass media research, or urban studies, in some cases crossing interdisciplinary lines and in other cases pioneering in areas like the sociology of work, of law, of education, and of the armed forces and society.

We needed a vehicle or a series of vehicles that would enable social scientists to inform each other, as well as generations of future students, about what was going on and how exciting it was. And so, the building of that vehicle became part of our reason for being, leading to an expansion of our book program, as well as the development of new journals. We did this with the help of many door-openers (or "gatekeepers") who published with us and brought us into contact with others in their networks.

My association with the eminent sociologist James S. Coleman (Jim) and his students, for example, led to the launch of an early journal, *Simulation &*

Gaming (originally *Simulation & Games*) in the early 1970s. Jim was noted for his work in the sociology of education and was still in the Chicago area when we met him. We knew him initially because of George's prior Free Press association (later on Jim went to Johns Hopkins). Jim was the author of the renowned Coleman Report, which studied educational equality in the United States and became a catalyst for desegregation. Jim opened an early door for us when he brought graduate students to us who were interested in editing and writing for *Simulation & Gaming*. We had at least one successful book in that area, as well. Today, we have two journals representing that field, one based in the United States and the other published from SAGE London.

These kinds of connections fostered the rapid growth of our publishing program. By the mid-1980s, similar long-term relationships with leading sociologists led to the realization that there was no comprehensive post–World War II handbook in the field of sociology. We saw this as both a challenge and an opportunity, and never ones to ignore either of those, we began a search for an editor and contributors for the project (which was also fueled ultimately by sheer curiosity about what was going on in sociology and where it was heading). This led to the publication of *The Handbook of Sociology*, edited by Neil Smelser in 1988, which was a landmark in the field of sociology at the time.

Many academics in these newly emerging fields and subfields in the social sciences established separate associations, such as the American Society of Criminology or the multidisciplinary International Communication Association. Soon researchers emerged who were more interested in the applications—the nuts and bolts of these fields—and they began publishing criminal justice studies to explore how the criminal justice system really worked. Another example was family studies, and working with the National Council of Family Relations led us to authors who were analyzing child abuse and domestic violence. People like Richard Gelles, now Dean of the School of Social Work at the University of Pennsylvania, published his first book with us, *The Violent Home*. Rich did his Ph.D. in sociology with Murray Straus at the University of New Hampshire. Both Rich and Murray were key pioneers in family violence research and introduced us to others in the field. We soon became a vital resource in this area for both researchers and practitioners and launched the *Journal of Interpersonal Violence*.

Sharing a Vision

Because of this burgeoning movement and our connection to it, George and I attended every sociology convention from the early 1970s on, meeting people and networking with important academics in the many subfields. We attended regional sociology meetings and were publishers for many years for the Pacific Sociological Association, working with so many wonderful people in the field of sociology and related multidisciplinary areas. It was the best of times.

We shared with these scholars a common vision that we would often discuss with regard to the original purpose and mission for SAGE Publications. As a result of our discussions, we would frequently use special issues of the *American Behavioral Scientist* (*ABS*) to do market research or test ideas for new journals. We had acquired *American Behavioral Scientist* before moving to California, back in the autumn of 1965, our second journal after *UAQ* (it is still one of SAGE's flagship journals today). Each issue was edited by a distinguished scholar who was developing cutting-edge materials on an emerging part of his or her field.

In many cases, those *ABS* special issue editors ultimately envisioned starting their own journals, and among the many "spin-off" journals we launched in this way were *Small Group Behavior* (originally called *Comparative Group Studies*), *Communication Research, Simulation & Gaming, Youth & Society,* and other titles in the late 1960s and 1970s and into the 1980s. Early on, we did a special issue edited by the late F. Gerald Kline (another Jerry) on research methods that were newly developing for analysis in the fields of mass communication and communication studies. The test issue went so well, it led to the establishment of an entire publishing program of books and journals in the field of communication research.

In 1969, we had begun publishing the journal *Criminology,* for the American Society of Criminology. Criminology as a field was more established than communication, but the side of criminology that applied research to the criminal justice system and penology was new and growing rapidly. It also linked to larger studies of law and society, as well as to domestic violence, child abuse, and elder abuse. It served as a model for a number of fields like communication that drew researchers from multiple disciplines and often became separate fields. For example, communication research was done by sociologists, social psychologists, and people with degrees from journalism schools and other programs. Today there are many departments and even schools of communication at numerous universities.

Subsequently, we also began publishing in the field of cross-cultural studies, and again, we did a very successful book in that field that became something of an advanced textbook. This encouraged us not only to do more in building our cross-cultural studies program and offerings but to make sure that we emphasized research methods and techniques that provided the best results and robust analyses for the minimum amount of money. Cross-cultural research was and is very expensive, and even then, grant money from foundations or the government to support it was challenging to get because the environment was so competitive.

Urban Studies Research

One of the earliest areas of research in social sciences that we helped to grow into a legitimate field was the area of urban studies. Urban research and urban studies was not a separate discipline in the middle of the 20th century but rather was taught as a subtopic in sociology and political science departments. Originally, sociologists were doing what is now called urban sociology, and political scientists were in separate departments teaching and doing research on state and local government, and a few other people were looking at what was to become urban anthropology or urban history. There were also separate departments of urban planning at major universities in the United States, Canada, the UK, and Europe.

Urban studies as a distinct field came into its own with Lyndon Johnson's Great Society in the mid-1960s, and our journal, *Urban Affairs Quarterly,* launched in 1965, was a part of that trend (see Chapter 1 in reference to Marilyn Gittell). So was the newsletter *Urban Research News,* started a few year later and for which I was the first editor, until we hired a part-time staff member to do it. Ultimately, so much material was coming out elsewhere that we didn't need to continue the newsletter.

The *Urban Affairs Annual Review* was an annual book series, the first of many we started, publishing at least 20 volumes in as many years analyzing different aspects of urban affairs. Libraries kept them on standing order, the book equivalent of a subscription, except payable on publication, not in advance. Still, it guaranteed a floor for revenues. Then, depending on the subject in the title, we could sell additional volumes to specialists. If we were lucky in selecting the topic and the editors pulled together a strong, coherent volume, we would also get sales as adoptions (textbook sales for graduate courses, perhaps 10 or 15 copies per order).

Leo Schnore was the co-editor of the first volume in the *Urban Affairs Annual Reviews*. I recall tramping across the snow at the University of Wisconsin in January (snow getting in the tops of my boots, because in those days boots didn't go up to the knees) to plot out both Volume 1, entitled *Urban Research and Policy Planning,* and the overall vision for the series, while kicking around suggestions to fill out the Editorial Advisory Board and other topics in the cold of a midwestern winter (which was, in those days, very cold indeed, although also very beautiful).

We started a number of these kinds of annual series in the 1970s and continued them into the 1980s. There was the *Sage Annual Reviews in Communication Research,* for example, that Jerry Kline and Peter Clarke served as series editors, with volume editors like Ellen Wartella, Gerald R. (Gerry) Miller, Jay Blumler, Elihu Katz, and Steven H. Chaffee, which had a tremendous impact and also helped us network widely, deeply, and rapidly into the field. We published more than 10 volumes in that series, which launched in the early 1970s and was published well into the 1980s. The series, as much as the journal Jerry and Peter launched (*Communication Research,* which is still one of our flagship journal titles), established us and our list. We designed the series so that each volume would give an overview of the state of the field in different subspecialties: mass communication, political communication, nonverbal interaction, persuasion, interpersonal communication, and so forth.

In urban and regional studies, as we were developing our lists, we were not just selling the journal and the *Urban Affairs Annual Reviews,* which came out once a year. We also took over, along with the *American Behavioral Scientist,* a bibliographic series, the *ABS Guide* and its annual supplement, *New Studies in the Social and Behavioral Sciences.* Each year we'd gather up what we had published as a special section of the *ABS* journal and release it to libraries as a slim bound book. (The original *ABS Guide* was quite fat since it covered about a decade.) College and reference librarians were buying bibliographies such as the *ABS Guide* series for library collections, and municipal reference libraries were buying urban specific bibliographies, including two we issued for that market (bibliographies on county government and on planning).

For a time, from 1965 to 1975, we were one of the main sources for what was going on in urban studies, which had grown out of various other fields. We got the corner on the first journals and books—not just *UAQ,* but also the British journal *Urban Studies,* which SAGE London now publishes.

When *Urban Studies* moved back to SAGE London in 2008, it was something of a homecoming for us. The originating publisher, Oliver & Boyd in Scotland, now a subsidiary of a UK publishing company, had pulled it back from SAGE, Inc. years before. The celebration party I attended in London was like a family reunion. I had originally built the journal's North American circulation base when SAGE, Inc. had the distribution rights, raising it from 5 to more than 300 subscribers in the United States and Canada during the early 1970s. At the party, I went around shaking the editors' hands, because I'd helped to put their feet solidly on the ground "this side of the pond" when that journal was just getting launched in the 1970s. It was definitely a walk down memory lane!

This is an example of the kind of support we gave in many fields, such as criminal justice and criminology, sociology, political science, international studies, and communication, over the past 45 years. Our authors and editors are very special to us, and we stay connected, and in some cases reconnected, with scores of journals and scholarly societies. We grew with them (and they with us), which is why we see our company as their "natural home." (Another journal that followed the pattern of *Urban Studies* was the *International Political Science Review,* which we launched in 1980 and published until 1986, and then began publishing again in 1996 when it returned to the SAGE family.)

Developing a Philosophy

As we went along in the process of building fields and building our lists, we developed a philosophy that guided our approach. First we developed a core journal and then built a good relationship with not just an editor but the editorial board members who had both stature and reputation in those fields. (A good example is how Stephen Barr of SAGE London did this with *Theory, Culture & Society;* see Chapter 9.) Then we figured out who the key players were in that field, especially those who shared our philosophy and our vision for the field or the subfield, and worked with them to expand our list.

We used this approach very successfully in the area of family studies and research, which ultimately led us to becoming one of the world's most, if not *the* world's most, notable publishers in the area of family violence, child abuse, and elder abuse ("granny bashing" in London). Our *Journal of Interpersonal Violence* was started in that area, and from that little acorn, a pretty significant tree grew.

We followed the same approach in other areas, often mining the field for people who would ultimately become major players. In 1971, when we started publishing in the field of communication, Jerry Kline and Peter Clarke were the "young Turks." Sandra Ball-Rokeach had become a key player in communications when I met her much later, in 1986. She was quite a bit more established at the time, because she had done some brilliant and pioneering work on the relationship between mass media and violence with George Gerbner, who was a member of the establishment in communication studies at the time of JFK's assassination. But Sandra is also a visionary, an excellent scholar and teacher. She was also the co-author of one of the bestselling texts in the field of communication when we met. Sandra is still a close friend and (along with Marilyn Gittell) a long-serving, insightful member of the McCune Foundation's Board of Directors.

What we were finding out was that we were encountering scholars from a new generation in field after field who had a different and expanded vision of their areas of scholarship. We helped them to transform and become a part of the establishment in each of their fields by publishing journals that put their feet solidly on the ground. We did this in field after field, subdiscipline after subdiscipline.

Another example of this approach was in the work done by Marvin Wolfgang, a well-known sociologist at the University of Pennsylvania who did trailblazing studies on gangs, juvenile violence, and juvenile recidivism in America. He also worked with a number of Europeans—especially in England and in Italy—so there was an international tinge to his work that fit in well with our own ambitions to "go global."

One of Marvin Wolfgang's collaborators in the international research on juvenile delinquency was Franco Ferracuti. He lived under conditions of tight security, because his work was so sensitive and controversial at the time. He had a huge dog and an iron door behind the wooden front entrance to his home. I remember our visiting Franco at Marvin's suggestion when George and I were in Rome selling translations to ERI, a publishing program that was attached to the radio and television company of Italy, because they were interested in the Italian rights to some of our communication books. Professor Wolfgang was also the president of the American Academy of Political and Social Science (AAPSS), whose journal (*Annals of the American Academy of Political and Social Science*) we have proudly published for decades. This kind of overlap was also true of many of our authors in communication and media studies, as well as in many other areas in the social sciences.

In this way, we eventually got to know a lot of the key players in Northern Europe, whether they were in the UK, the Netherlands, or Scandinavia, which is how we acquired Denis McQuail's book *Mass Communication Theory,* now in its 6th edition. There were people who were keen to do international research and see if the same patterns would emerge in multiple countries, as they did in political science and in international studies. We certainly used that trend to our advantage, as well (see Chapter 9 for more developments in the UK and Europe).

Gender Studies

It could be fairly said that SAGE and the field of gender studies were born together. Forty-five years ago, a student in the social and behavioral sciences would have found no courses on gender in the catalog, other than a course on marriage and the family tucked away in sociology. Today, gender studies and women's studies are mainstays of every college and university, and SAGE's many journals and edited collections of research and policy recommendations in gender studies helped legitimate and sustain the development of those fields.

One pioneering effort back in the late 1970s and early 1980s was an annual series of edited books, *SAGE Yearbooks in Women's Policy Studies* (seven volumes). I worked closely with the editors of these volumes (and played a similar role in other series), often convincing them to change their titles for more marketability. The titles in that series became, for example, *Economic Independence for Women: The Foundation for Equal Rights;*

Women Into Wives: The Legal and Economic Impact of Marriage; The Victimization of Women; Working Women and Families; Women and Household Labor; Women's Retirement: Policy Implications of Recent Research; and the final volume in 1983, *Women in Washington: Advocates for Public Policy.*

We published some award-winning books that sold very well, including Marcia Guttentag's *Too Many Women?* Many volumes in the SAGE Library of Social Research series were on topics within women's studies and family studies, although this was a series that included more than 125 volumes (which were published over more than a decade), and many fields were included (criminology, politics, and communication—to name just a few).

Gender studies was almost entirely concerned with women, but in 1985, Michael Kimmel (currently professor of sociology, SUNY Stony Brook) met with Mitch Allen and pitched his idea of starting a new journal on a new subfield, the subject of men. We tested the idea in a special issue of *American Behavioral Scientist,* which resulted in an anthology he edited, entitled *Changing Men: New Directions in Research on Men and Masculinity* (1987), which remains a solid seller today. A book series followed, *SAGE Series on Men and Masculinities* (15 volumes), and then finally, a scholarly journal, *Men and Masculinities,* all edited by Kimmel.

We have continued to publish on gender studies to the present with notable titles, including those in the series *Women and Work: A Research and Policy Series* (six volumes) starting in 1997 and the *Handbook of Studies on Men and Masculinities* (2004), co-edited by Michael Kimmel with two other scholars from Britain and Australia. We did a lot more in gender studies early on, as well, producing edited volumes that crossed disciplines with original essays in the SAGE Focus Editions (titles like *Black Women, Black Men, Black Families*), as well as many highly respected journals in both gender studies and ethnic studies.

Comparative Politics

Comparative politics was another area in which we did early work. When we found ourselves without an editor-in-chief for the journal *Comparative Political Studies,* I became the founding managing editor. This was a similar situation to my being the editor of *Urban Research News,* and I also served as managing editor of *American Behavioral Scientist* for quite a few years (but now we have Laura Lawrie doing that job, based in Arizona and working with a terrific group of editorial advisory board members that she developed over the past two decades).

The editorial board of *Comparative Political Studies,* over time, played a key role in bringing us many of the Goods and the Greats (people who shaped the field) in that area—Gabriel Almond, Harry Eckstein, and Sidney Verba, to name a few. Irving Louis Horowitz was a sociologist who made significant contributions in comparative research. Irv was a giant of a man and at one point had founded a magazine originally called *Transaction* (it was rebaptized at my suggestion to *Society*). We published a series edited by him called *Studies in Comparative International Development,* but the books had an 8.5 × 11–inch trim size (not 5.5 × 8.5 inches like the other SAGE Papers). They were available on subscription and individually as part of the great SAGE "papers caper" (see Chapter 3). Horowitz also edited a book for us in which his generation of Greats in sociology gave their views of what sociology was all about and where the field was going. Karl Deutsch, at Columbia University, was another one of the comparative political studies Greats. A past president of the American Political Science Association, Karl was unfailingly generous with his time, insights, and advice.

Opening Gates in the Midwest

We did much of our best work in the social sciences with the major state universities of the Midwest and not so much, originally, with the Ivy League schools (although we always had board members on various journals who were from the Ivy League universities). While all of our advisory editors and journal boards gave us an incredible amount of information and guidance, opening doors for us right and left, scholars at the "Big 10" in the Midwest, including schools such as the University of Michigan, the University of Illinois, and the University of Iowa, were even more forthcoming in terms of actually having us publish their books, not just their journal articles. They were very proactive (as were public university faculty throughout the United States and the UK), and many of them signed with us because they were impressed with our marketing approaches. Together, we built lists in their fields and developed deep and influential relationships, teaching us at the same time we were helping them and their students. Some very solid bonds were forged in those first decades of building SAGE.

At the University of Michigan, Warren Miller and his colleagues were doing research on American politics while simultaneously blazing trails in survey research and other research methodology. The joke between Warren and me was that we were related—"kissing cousins"—because even though he was a big shot in the American Political Science Association when I was still running around in miniskirts in the 1960s, we would frequently kiss each other on the cheek as a form of greeting.

I recall a time when, fairly early on in my career, I traveled to Michigan to meet Warren so he could introduce me to potential authors at the university. I was planning to find out what research they were doing, what topics would be the focus of the seminars on research methods that they ran during summer breaks at the university, and to get advice on needed publications.

I arrived on short notice, having made an arrangement to meet Warren at a restaurant in Ann Arbor. But when he arrived, he let me know that he deserved a medal for meeting with me. I asked what the medal was for, and he replied, "Don't you know that today is the day of 'the game?'" I had no idea what he was talking about but later found out that Michigan was playing Ohio State that day. Warren met with me for a brief period (no one else on the social science faculty at the University of Michigan would meet with me that day) and then went off to see the football game. At that point in my life, I had never been to a football game because my college, Queens College, part of the City University of New York, didn't have a football team. To while away the time, I visited a friend's daughter who was a student (and more interested in biology than football) and toured Ann Arbor's bookstores before visiting other authors on Monday and then heading back to California.

The Michigan Mafia (as I nicknamed them) were very much a part of building SAGE in the early days. Many of them were in political science, and I got to know them first through Warren. They did amazing research and were key players in the field of American politics (as well as comparative politics). There were also incredible sociologists, like Beverly Duncan and Otis Dudley Duncan, both of whom were especially significant for their work in the field of demographics. Many of the these researchers had also been Free Press authors and were still unhappy that it had been subsumed into Macmillan—thereby losing what Jerry Kaplan had brought to them when the company was independent. George had known them from the time he was director of the Free Press, and so we developed close ties with them and others at the "Big 10" public universities in the Midwest.

Another key Midwest contact of George's from the Free Press was Peter Rossi, who was at the University of Chicago and ultimately became president of the American Sociological Association, as did his wife, Alice Rossi, a few years after him. Pete was the co-author of our best-selling text, *Evaluation*, which is now in its 7th edition. Today he's Professor Emeritus of Sociology at the University of Massachusetts.

One year, we were on a very tight publishing schedule for *Evaluation* (a little over two months to get from manuscript to bound book), and I remember calling Peter up on Christmas day to tell him I needed his edits on the page proofs for the first edition of *Evaluation* either that day or the very next. He told me he was cleaning house for the holidays and couldn't do it at that moment but would call me first thing the next day. And he did. The book went on to be a best seller and a perfect exemplar of what an intelligent advanced textbook should be: clear, well written, with mini–case studies illustrating best practices in the field. Pete Rossi and Howie Freeman did a brilliant job with that text. Pete had been head of the National Opinion Research Center (NORC) at the University of Chicago, and he and James S. Coleman were incredible in terms of opening doors for us in the field of sociology.

Morris Janowitz, another Free Press contact and Midwest pioneer in what ultimately became the field of urban studies, became a valuable adviser to us within a year of starting the company. As I have mentioned, urban sociology was a subtopic within departments of sociology in those days—not yet what Marilyn Gittell and her colleagues envisioned. But by the time *Urban Affairs Quarterly* was founded, Morris Janowitz had moved on to a new area that he helped create with other sociologists and political scientists, which became the focus of our journal *Armed Forces & Society*. Morris became a door-opener for us for all sorts of things, and a valued adviser. His wife and daughters were also gracious.

Pete Rossi, along with Morris Janowitz and Jim Coleman, were key people early on who introduced us to potential authors and editors throughout the Midwest at major public universities, as well as to scholars at the University of Chicago. This was all part of a huge network going on in these disciplines, and George and I were discovering many new frontiers within these subfields. The contribution of these men and other door-openers (and "gate-keepers") was extremely valuable. The "invisible colleges" in a field (or a subfield) are always where the action is!

Because we did so much work with Morris Janowitz and George had other Free Press contacts in the area, I don't think we'd ever visited Chicago without George bringing me to Evanston (a suburb of Chicago). It was on such visits that I got to know Tom Cook, who was a former graduate student and collaborator with the brilliant Donald Campbell. Tom Cook did the famous evaluation study of *Sesame Street* that was actually replicated in Mexico (because the show had also played in Latin America). People like Tom, who can think creatively and also explain their ideas to multiple generations of students both by teaching them in small graduate classes and by reaching them through books, are valuable role models. They excite and inspire students. They also open up new roads for others to travel on. Tom and Faye (his wife) are very good at that, as well as being remarkable and respected researchers. Tom is now also a fellow of the American Academy of Political and Social Science.

We stayed in touch with Don Campbell throughout the latter part of his life, not only at Northwestern University (as part of our Chicago visits) but also when he was at Syracuse University before he died. Tom continued to work with Don on research methodology, and they also collaborated on much pathbreaking work in evaluation together. Don was an outstanding social psychologist, one of those people who were always curious and would read about everything, and could somehow come up with new ideas that included nuggets from the past—but also reached far into the future. I had first met him (by letter even before we finally met face-to-face) when he agreed to serve on the *ABS* editorial board. His advice was unfailingly helpful, and his insight and comments on unmet needs in the social and behavioral sciences were extraordinarily prescient.

Influencing Future Generations

In mentioning great scholars like Don Campbell and Tom Cook, I want to emphasize and acknowledge that they both nurtured wonderful students, many of whom subsequently followed them as splendid researchers and teachers. They were great pioneers in influencing new research in their fields.

And what we observed with many of "the Greats," as we did with Gabriel Almond at Stanford and Sid Verba at Harvard (with Almond and Verba, the research focus was comparative politics), was a similar insight into the behavior(s) they researched, as well as the networking magic of their names.

Gabriel Almond (a past president of the American Political Science Association) and Sid Verba were also like this, influencing generations to come through their graduate students in comparative politics. Gabe was one of those people who was a gentlemen and a scholar, like Harry Eckstein at Princeton. I didn't know Sid Verba as well, not having spent as much time with him, but Almond and Eckstein were influential and active members on the board of *Comparative Political Studies* while I was serving as managing editor of the journal and getting it off the ground. They were invaluable at giving advice, opening doors, and encouraging us to explore the work of their graduate students, who themselves became stars in their field subsequently. They wrote beautifully and expected the same from others.

What we found these people all had in common, whether they were in politics or sociology, was that they had left their marks on multiple parts of their disciplines or created new interdisciplinary fields. While being such intellectual pioneers, they also encouraged their students to become intellectual pioneers, as well. Richard D. Schwartz, or "Red" Schwartz, as he was known (for his red hair, which turned white more than a decade ago!), was one of these, the founding editor of the journal *Law & Society*. He was a very good friend, originally at Northwestern, and a pioneer in creating that field, just as Morris Janowitz had been a pioneer in creating *Armed Forces & Society*.

People hadn't been looking at such areas before World War II, not in such a rigorous and yet intellectually creative way. In many cases, as with Marilyn Gittell, the founding editor of *Urban Affairs Quarterly,* we were working in areas where it was so rich because different disciplines were overlapping and, in doing so, creating a tremendous ferment of new ideas to open up new pathways, not just for the scholars but also for at least a generation or two of their students (who then went off and became pioneers and leaders in their own right).

At SAGE, we were playing a key role in many of these fields, which is why we (and our advisers) are sometimes referred to as "gatekeepers."

CHAPTER 7

Growing Wider and Deeper

More About the Greats (and the Goods, Too!)

One of the best parts of my entire career has been the opportunity to interact over the decades with brilliant people. In so many cases, these people
were also incredibly good human beings, and it was a pleasure and a privilege to know them. I miss not being in the field these recent decades,
because I've lost frequent contact with many of the folks I always thought of
as the Goods and the Greats. Many were scholars who courageously established new areas of intellectual territory during their careers. Others were
"public intellectuals" or friends from the world of publishing. Unfortunately,
having moved into more managerial activities, I'm not as often in touch with
old friends—except when they get honored or buried. I sometimes feel as if
I've spoken at a few too many memorial services, but I certainly enjoy celebrating the honors achieved by people I've known since "way back when."

Many of these friends were introduced in Chapter 6, but I wish to honor
still more of them in this chapter by including brief references to their accomplishments and their association with me and SAGE.

Many People Helped Us Grow

Al de Grazia founded the *American Behavioral Scientist* with Heinz Eulau
(and at least one other political scientist I did not know) on the West Coast,

and Al took it over when he moved to New York City. The journal was called by a different name during the first three years—*PROD* for *Political Research Organization and Design.* Al would say to me (and probably to anyone else who would listen) that "a journal is the greatest calling card in the world."

I have found that to be absolutely true. There were so many great scholars I met by introducing myself as the publisher of *Urban Affairs Quarterly* or the *American Behavioral Scientist.* I often met them at the American Sociological Association or the American Political Science Association (or from the mid-1970s onwards at the American Psychological Association) conventions because of this "in."

Al also introduced me to **Harold Lasswell**, one of the leading American political scientists of his generation. At one time, he served as president of the American Political Science Association. Professor Lasswell was admittedly older when I lunched with him in Manhattan but still incredibly insightful, and even though sometimes hard to follow, he had a wonderful and creative way of looking at all things political.

I originally met **Daniel Patrick Moynihan (Pat),** who preceded Hillary Clinton in the role of senior senator from New York (before she became Secretary of State for President Obama), when he was the head of the Joint Center for Urban Studies at MIT and Harvard. When Pat was on the faculty at Harvard, he was very helpful in getting me access to the prime movers in urban affairs and urban studies at the time we were launching *UAQ* in the mid-1960s. Pat embodied much of what the American Academy of Political and Social Science (AAPSS) felt should be the standard for the great scholars and policy makers in the United States, people who, if their fields weren't political science or sociology, would be eligible for a Nobel Prize.

Because of people like Pat Moynihan, the Academy wanted to establish a significant award, alternating annually between an academic and a policy maker. Sometimes, the recipient might have had a career that spanned both categories, as Moynihan's did. I was on the Academy's Board at the time (I still am, as of this writing), and we decided to name the award the Moynihan Prize. SAGE and I contributed to that prize, and I also raised other monies from Pat's former students, friends, colleagues, and family. The third award will be made in May 2010, in Washington, D.C.

Pat Moynihan is widely known as the author of the Moynihan Report, written under then President Nixon, which reported on black families in the same way James Coleman reported the inequalities of separate but equal education in the Coleman Report. Pat was reviled for openly discussing the terrible havoc being caused in our urban communities because of the absence of black fathers in black families. And of course, both reports were very controversial for scholars to do. But they were also very important and needed to be presented to our government and to all voters for public discussion and policy making. In fact, the American Academy of Political and Social Science recently published an issue of their journal, *The Annals* (January 2009), after they held a conference on "The Moynihan Report Re-visited," some 50 years after the report had been done.

James S. Rosenau (Jim) was a good friend whom we knew originally when he was teaching comparative foreign policy at the University of Southern California and we were publishing journals and books for the International Studies Association. Jim and George had a lot in common, both being roughly the same age and having been through the latter part of World War II, and they could both recall President Roosevelt's funeral cortege. I remember one Sunday morning the three of us were having brunch in a restaurant on South Beverly Drive when Jim suddenly turned to our waiter and said, "I know you, I know your face. You were that man in the photograph, sitting on the street curb, crying at Roosevelt's funeral." The waiter was a big man, built like a football player, but on hearing Jim's words, he practically burst into tears again. It was amazing that Jim had recognized the man and that both he and George recalled the photo. When Jim moved back east to teach in Washington, D.C., I did not see him as often. But I remember him as being both sensitive and very insightful.

Advancements in Methods

Many other Goods and Greats that I got to know and work with in the field of evaluation and in methodology deserve admiring mention. One of these was **Marcia Guttentag**, who died too young of a heart attack, and her co-editor, **Elmer "Moose" Streuning**, both top-ranking social psychologists who were the co-editors of the *Handbook of Evaluation Research*, which we published in a two-volume set. Marcia, Moose, and the chapter authors had produced the work under a major federal grant from the National Institutes of Mental Health, working with a group of incredible social scientists. They donated the royalties for the *Handbook* to the Society for Psychological Studies and Social Issues (SPSSI). I recall that after Marcia saw the first royalty statements for the two-volume *Handbook,* she said, "If I'd known you were going to sell that many, I would have taken part of the royalty—I could have sent both my kids to Harvard on that much!"

It was a similar situation with the first edition of the *Program Evaluation Kit,* which we did in eight volumes and then shipped in a cardboard box. But with the second edition, we were more sophisticated and had a custom-made box for the nine-volume set that went inside the shipping box. The UCLA Graduate School of Education put together the *Program Evaluation Kit,* and because we'd been so successful with the *Handbook,* they came to us with the *Kit.* The conditions of the government grant that funded development of the *Kit* mandated that any royalty money was to go back to the research center at the Graduate School of Education at UCLA, where the work had been developed. The authors of the *Kit* knew that going in, whereas Marcia had no idea how well we'd do on sales of the *Handbook.*

But by the time we did the *Program Evaluation Kit,* we were "the" publishers in the field of evaluation, having launched many new publications, including a journal and several top-selling books. I was not surprised when we passed the $1 million mark in sales of the *Kit,* and we ultimately did a lot more than that with both the *Handbook* and the *Kit.* I don't know, if another publisher had had the *Handbook* on their list, that they could have marketed it the way we did and have had the same results. We'll never know, but the kind of direct mail lists that we had access to would have been difficult (if not impossible) for another publisher to obtain. Then we also had the mailing lists of our buyers, which we had developed in-house. In addition, we had access to several lists that we obtained via our authors and the sponsoring society. A larger publisher's marketing department would not necessarily have followed up as keenly and worked so closely with the editors (and their responses to our marketing questionnaire and follow-up phone calls).

But as so often was the case in the early risks we took (publishing in newly developing areas or with new groups of younger authors), we were indeed betting the store, and so were willing to do the work we thought was necessary in marketing and sales for widest possible dissemination. We were also genuinely swept away in the enthusiasm of our editors and authors over what they were doing and how their research could be used for the betterment of society. Publishers can get almost as messianic about their projects as their authors do, picking up the bug from interacting with them.

Then, down the road, I can't help but remember that we had incredible good fortune in getting to know such terrific people who were making huge and notable contributions to their respective fields. In evaluation, I think of people like **Pete Rossi, Howie Freeman, Dick Berk, Don Campbell,** and **Tom Cook.** It should, of course, be noted that I often got to know many of them as they were wearing multiple hats. Don Campbell and Tom Cook were well known for their brilliant and lasting contributions to research methodology, as well as their work in evaluation studies, for example. And then when I think about the people who got the "little green books" off the ground—**Chris Achen, Michael Lewis-Beck, Larry Mayer, John Sullivan, Rick Uslaner,** and **Ron Webber** (to name them in alphabetical order)—to conceptualize and then actualize the vision was a pretty amazing achievement.

When you add the people over the years who have worked not just with me but with our brilliant acquisition editors (like **C. Deborah Laughton** and **Mitch Allen** in California and **Chris Rojek** in London, to name just a few), it really takes my breath away. Our journal editors and editorial boards offered good advice and helped us network. They often were the ones to remind us that we should be looking at quantitative techniques, qualitative techniques, applied social research, and mixed methods—and to think about where these areas could make contributions on widely differing subjects and topics. With such remarkable editors, editorial boards, and authors, we were wonderfully gifted and helped at every turn.

Gareth Morgan is Distinguished Research Professor at York University in Toronto, where he teaches at the Schulich School of Business. Like the late George McCune, Gareth is truly a gentleman and a scholar. His contributions to management thinking have brought him many international awards, including election as Life Fellow of the International Academy of Management in recognition of an outstanding contribution to the science of management. His books published with SAGE include *Beyond Method: Strategies for Social Research* (1983); *Images of Organization* (1986); *Creative*

Organization Theory: A Resourcebook (1989); *Teaching Organization Theory: An Instructor's Manual* (1989); *Imaginization: New Mindsets for Seeing, Organizing, and Managing* (1993); and the classic *Images of Organization* (2nd edition, 1997).

A Celebration in Words: SAGE 1965–2005

Gareth Morgan, *Distinguished Research Professor, York University, Toronto*

From the moment I met George McCune at the SAGE bookstand located in a warm open-air booth at a sociology conference in Mexico City in 1981, I knew that I was dealing with a very special kind of publisher—one who was genuinely interested in new ideas and in taking chances with authors who felt that they had something to say. I left the conversation with George with a warm, positive feeling that I had made contact with a person who genuinely wanted me to keep in touch as my work progressed, to see if SAGE could be of help.

As time went on, I quickly realized that what I had experienced in that conversation went far beyond George, and that in working with SAGE I would gradually become a member of an extended publishing family that embraced many other members of the firm and fellow authors. I soon had conversations with Sara, realized that SAGE stood for <u>SA</u>ra and <u>GE</u>orge in far more than name, and that their enthusiasm for books, ideas and pushing the boundaries of academic publishing into new territory was what the company was really all about. Under the continued leadership of Sara, David, and editors who often got as excited about a book as the author, the company went from strength to strength.

For many academics and other social science professionals, SAGE's regular announcements of new titles became a valuable way of getting an early global view of what was happening in their field. If you look at the publishing record, SAGE's list of titles shows that the company has been at the leading edge of many innovative trends in the social sciences and has consistently taken risks that were way in advance of what many journal editors were prepared to take. Take, for example, early SAGE contributions to the development of innovative research methodology, research on organizational culture, gender and organization, critical organization studies, education research and criminology—to name just a few.

SAGE stands in a niche of its own when compared with many other publishing companies, because Sara, David and colleagues have been passionate about pushing the boundaries in terms of what's possible. Instead of just serving established markets on the basis of safe "rearview mirror" market research, they took the chance with new ideas that they felt could make a positive difference. They got the ideas out there—early! And if you want to change a field, that's what ultimately counts.

Communication Studies

Some of the Goods and the Greats were noted for their advancements in research methodology and were giants in their field (as described in the previous chapter). Many were in communication studies, such as **Elihu Katz** and his Israeli colleagues at Hebrew University in Jerusalem. Elihu's area was mass communication, especially the mass media (he also served as consultant on broadcasting research to the Israeli equivalent of the BBC), his main focus being the interplay between media, opinion, and action in the public sphere. Elihu is Trustee Professor at the Annenberg School for Communication, University of Pennsylvania; Emeritus Professor of Sociology and Communication at the Hebrew University of Jerusalem; and Scientific Director of the Guttman Institute of Applied Social Research. Elihu is a winner of the UNESCO-Canada McLuhan Prize, the Burda Prize (in media research), and other distinctions, including honorary degrees from the Universities of Ghent, Montreal, Paris, and Haifa.

Christine Borgman is Professor and Presidential Chair in Information Studies at the Graduate School of Education and Information Studies, UCLA, and the author of more than 180 publications in the fields of information studies, computer science, and communication. She is best known for her work in scholarly communication, scientific information, and bibliometrics (methods used to study or measure texts and information). Her degree from the University of Pittsburgh was in library science originally, and she met her husband, George Mood, a recently retired law librarian, at Stanford while she was getting her Ph.D. in Communications. Chris does a lot of research and speaking now on how scholars use the Internet in doing their research and their teaching, not just in the United States but also in the UK and Eastern Europe. This is a field that changes rapidly, as one would expect. Chris is one of the experts who is nearly always at the cutting edge.

From Scholar to University Administrator

Judith Rodin was a highly regarded member of a younger generation of social psychologists when I first met her. She was very helpful in broadening our social psychology list beyond evaluation. She subsequently became a well-known administrator, serving as President of the University of Pennsylvania from 1994 to 2004, the first woman to become the president of an Ivy League school. Dr. Rodin has been serving as President of the Rockefeller Foundation since 2005.

Amy Gutman is a distinguished communication scholar and the current president of the University of Pennsylvania, following Judith Rodin as the eighth president in 2004. A respected social scientist, she is another example of the remarkable female scholars we published early in their careers who went on to become highly regarded scholars and then path-breaking university administrators. These include, in addition to Dr. Rodin, Ellen Wartella and Gretchen Bataille.

Ellen Wartella is a leading scholar in communications, studying the role of media in children's development. We actually published her first book (a terrific read on children's responses to TV advertising). She and her family have been friends ever since. Ellen and Chuck's older son is the same age as my grandson Doug. (Chuck is Professor Charles Whitney, who has also published many articles over the years on journalism with SAGE.) Ellen served as Executive Vice Chancellor and Provost at the University of California at Riverside from 2004 to 2009 and is currently Distinguished Professor of Psychology there. She was dean of the College of Communication at the University of Texas at Austin from 1993 to 2004, where she also held the Walter Cronkite Regents Chair, the Mary Gibbs Jones Centennial Chair, and the UNESCO Chair in International Communication.

Gretchen Bataille is a good friend of mine and now a member of the SAGE, Inc. Board of Directors. Gretchen became the fourteenth president of the University of North Texas in August 2006. She has served as a senior university administrator at Washington State University, the University of California at Santa Barbara, Arizona State University, and California State Polytechnic University at Pomona. A recognized scholar, Gretchen has focused on issues of diversity, civil rights, and ethnic studies throughout her professional career; her publications include books on Native American literature and film, as well as the role of administrators in higher education.

(John Wiemann is another scholar who became a university administrator; see Chapter 13, p. 175.)

Social Psychology

In the field of social psychology, there are so many I wish to mention, but here briefly are a few.

In the area of social psychology, **Milton Rokeach**, Sandra Ball-Rokeach's late husband, whom I met in 1976, was an influential star. He and Donald Campbell (see Chapter 5, p. 40) both did their graduate work at UC Berkeley under the GI Bill after World War II. Mendel (Milton's nickname) was the descendant of a long line of rabbis in Eastern Europe, and his parents were very disappointed when he hadn't continued that tradition. I always thought he did in a way, because a rabbi is a teacher, and Mendel was one of the great teachers of his generation in social psychology, as well as being a brilliant and creative thinker (as was Don Campbell) in that field. One of his great contributions, and some of the work he collaborated on with Sandra, was in understanding how Americans derived their core values, a terrific body of research.

Mendel also did great research in a number of other fields, including a brilliant study on delusional belief systems that was subsequently turned into a very popular book in the mid-1960s, titled *The Three Christs of Ypsilanti* (the movie rights have been secured, but I don't think the movie has or will be made). He had been consulting while doing his postdoctoral work for a mental health hospital in Ypsilanti, Michigan, where three schizophrenic in-patients each claimed to be Jesus Christ. The hospital staff had been keeping them in separate wards and on separate floors, but Mendel put the three together in the same ward and confronted them with each other's conflicting claims while encouraging them to interact personally as a support group. The book describes the outcome of his experiment and the changes he docu-mented in the patients' beliefs as a result. Absolutely brilliant thinking—and it's a great read, just beautifully written. But the movie options granted have not yet produced a workable script.

Elizabeth (Beth) Loftus is one of the most interesting people I know, as is her research on how to determine the accuracy of eyewitness testimony. The late **Hilde Himmelweit** was another one of the great pioneers in social psy-chology who became a main force in media studies, researching what can be learned from the effects of the mass media on society. **Elinor Langer** was instrumental in broadening our social psychology list beyond evaluation. She did fascinating studies on mindlessness versus mindful behavior—how a person could, for example, even be driving along in a car in a state of mindlessness. She also studied other states of consciousness, such as when people get older and become too dependent, causing them to lapse into a state that social psychologists call "learned helplessness."

I recall one summer, as I was traveling with Elinor to Cape Cod and we got stuck in traffic along the highway, we never even noticed the hours that went by—the conversation was so intense. I first met her through the *Handbook of Evaluation Research,* but we also kept in touch because we were publishing the *Personality and Social Psychology Bulletin (PSPB)* at the time (and still do). Our connection with social psychologists was not only with Division 8 of the American Psychological Association, which we'd originally bonded with because of the *Handbook of Evaluation Research,* but also with Division 9, for whom we publish the *PSPB.*

Work and Women

Among the many researchers and public intellectuals who changed our perceptions, I would include all of the following women, since I think they share common ground with regard to the issue of women's roles in society, including women in work, particularly in political work, and those who are running for office.

Betty Friedan was a writer, activist, and founder, along with Gloria Steinem, of feminism. Her 1963 book *The Feminine Mystique* is sometimes credited with sparking the "second wave" of feminism. Friedan co-founded and became the first president of the National Organization for Women in 1966, which aimed to bring women into equal partnerships with men. SAGE was a pioneer in the field of gender studies publishing, including an annual series of edited books, *SAGE Yearbooks in Women's Policy Studies* (seven volumes), in the late 1970s and early 1980s, with such topics as economic independence for women, legal and economic impact of marriage, working women and families, women and household labor, women's retirement, and women in politics (see Chapter 6 for more on how I worked closely with editors of this series).

On a personal note, Betty Friedan was also a friend of Jerry Kaplan's, so one spring break in the 1990s, the three of us went up to my cabin in

Yosemite together. During our stay, Betty took more of her asthma medica-tion than was safe at that altitude (despite her doctor's warnings) and went into congestive heart failure. I rushed her to the clinic in Oakhurst just south of the national park and she was subsequently transferred by ambulance to one of the major hospitals in Fresno. I then rushed back into Yosemite to save Jerry, who was diabetic (and in danger of going into diabetic shock) by get-ting some food prepared for him. Jerry Kaplan was of the generation of males who did not know how to cook (unless they were professional chefs). For years, he lived in New York City, dining at restaurants or bringing in gourmet goodies from some of the local shops in the tony area on the Upper East Side where he lived, just a bit north of the UN building. I left Betty at the clinic in the hands of an especially attentive nurse who'd been raised on *The Feminine Mystique* by her mother, obviously a devoted fan, as the nurse promised to give Betty extra good care! She did, and I was able to get both Jerry and Betty out of Yosemite alive!

Gloria Steinem and I have crossed paths twice, once when SAGE's *Journal of Black Studies* was being honored on its 20th anniversary by Temple University (where Molefi Asante had founded their graduate program in that field). She was a speaker at that event, along with the wonderful black actor Avery Brooks, who played the terrific (and favorite) character of Hawk in the television series *Spenser for Hire*. I met Gloria again late in 2008 when we were seated together at another dinner (this one was in New York). I was one of those honored by Women's Campaign International (WCI) at their first annual awards dinner. WCI is a group that provides advocacy training for women throughout the world. Our table was quite star-studded, with Hillary Clinton, Katie Couric, and Muriel Siebert, who recently celebrated her 40th anniversary as the first woman member of the New York Stock Exchange, joining Gloria Steinem, and a wonderful woman from Malawi who was rep-resenting their newly elected president (female) and serving as Malawi's Minister for Tourism and Trade (if I recall our conversation correctly).

Marjorie Margolies, the founder and head of WCI, is on the Faculty of the Fels Institute of Government at the University of Pennsylvania. She served one term as a member of the U.S. House of Representatives from Pennsylvania and was married to former Iowa Congressman Edward Mezvinsky. (Their son, Marc Mezvinsky, is currently engaged to Chelsea Clinton, who also attended the WCI honoring ceremonies in 2008.) I got to know Marjorie originally through both the American Academy of Political and Social Science and the Samuels Center in New York. In the summer of 2008, I spent more quality time with her and **Susan Rose**, former county supervisor in Santa Barbara and head of the Los Angeles Women's Rights Commission, at our family's lodge in Yosemite.

A Final Tribute

In my final reflections, I want to emphasize how tremendously indebted George and I were to Jerry Kaplan, who first identified many of our authors through his work with the Free Press. Jerry gave us incredible opportunities to work with the Goods and the Greats of social science. Through the years, these people not only opened doors for us but respected George's intelligence, his understanding, and especially his memory, because George never forgot a conversation. At scores of conventions we attended, I was the one who would say, "George, you remember professor so and so . . ." and George would then begin talking with whomever it was, picking up a conversation they'd had two, three, or five years earlier. Amazingly, George remembered those conversations as if they'd only just occurred the previous week!

Jerry Kaplan died of cancer in a New York hospital on August 10, 1993, at 67 years of age. I eulogized him in our company newsletter, *SAGE Thymes,* with the following words:

A Tribute to Jeremiah Kaplan

A distinguished publisher, Mr. Kaplan's career spanned nearly 50 years, during which time he founded two publishing companies, the Free Press and Meridian Books. Kaplan served as president of two large New York City–based publishing houses (Macmillan Publishing Company and Simon & Schuster, Inc.), as managing director of Cassell & Collier Macmillan, Ltd (a division of Macmillan, Inc.), and as president of the Association of American Publishers. He was active on the boards of a number of Jewish charities, as well as cultural and educational organizations. After his retirement from Simon & Schuster in 1989, he served as a consultant to the New York City Board of Education and consulted with and served as a board member of Scholastic, Inc. (which specializes in elementary–high school publishing).

(Continued)

(Continued)

Jerry Kaplan also served on the Board of Directors of SAGE Publications, Inc. for the last three years, as well as on the boards of two East Coast–based university presses (MIT and University of Pennsylvania). He was a valued friend and adviser to the late George D. McCune and Sara Miller McCune for 30 years, and more recently to David F. McCune, as well as to the executives of SAGE and its subsidiaries. His fellow Board members will miss his trenchant wit, pithy comments, unique insights, unparalleled experience, and invaluable publishing expertise.

As I noted at the start of this chapter, it is hard to speak of people in the past tense. Yet, the flip side of the coin would be never to have known them at all. That would never be an acceptable choice for many of us to make. Don't you, as a reader, agree?

PART III

Expanding Globally— Transforming at Home

CHAPTER 8

Going Global

SAGE India

With business in London running smoothly, George and I turned our thoughts to India in the late 1970s. I had never been to India but had friends there from my days at Pergamon Press. George had developed a fascination for the subcontinent while stationed in Karachi with the Army Air Corps (before it became the U.S. Air Force) during the last years of World War II.

By 1980, we felt secure enough in our growth and profitability to explore another joint international venture. To do so in India would be a long-term commitment, we believed, because we knew the Indian economy was not going to give us much in the way of profits for decades to come. Numerous other countries had been considered as foreign expansion alternatives, including Latin America, where we'd had relationships with various scholars and academic publishers, including some who had done translation agreements with us very successfully. I still spoke some Spanish and read it quite well, so I felt that with practice and exposure I could become reasonably fluent.

Our Latin American authors were all for it, but there were issues that still concerned us. Few people at SAGE in California could handle

Source: Text adapted with permission from Whiting, V. R., & Reardon, K. K. Strategic alliance in India: Sage Publications. In R. T. Moran, D. O. Braaten, & J. E. Walsh Jr. (Eds.), *International Business Case Studies for the Multicultural Marketplace* (pp. 62–69). Houston, TX: Gulf Publishing Company. Copyright © 1994 by Elsevier.

business in any foreign language (due to a flaw in the American educational system that still exists today). There were potential dangers in terms of currency instability and monetary black markets. There was *mordida* (bribery) to be considered, something we were adamantly opposed to. These problems of course existed in India, as well.

At that time, we also had some exceedingly influential Indian academics who were totally supportive of our entrance into Indian publishing, including Rajni Kothari (one of India's leading political scientists), T. N. ("Loki") Madan, an equally renowned sociologist, who was then the head of the Indian Social Science Research Council, and their colleagues at several of India's major universities and research centers.

In addition, David Brooks, late in his term as SAGE London's Managing Director, had set up a distribution agreement for SAGE's book products with Macmillan, Ltd (a different international publishing firm from the Crowell-Collier subsidiary Macmillan Inc) in India, and they had a very dynamic sales director in their Delhi office named Tejeshwar Singh. This was the very person named by our advisers in India as the perfect person to set up SAGE India!

In January 1980, George and I traveled to India together and met with several possible candidates for the lead role in a potential Indian venture. It was the first time I had visited the country, although I had many Indian friends from the UK and via Manu Chakravarty and her family, as well as our academic connections.

Several conditions at the time encouraged us to consider expanding to India. First, India had a huge population and was the second most populous country in the world at that time, with 700 million citizens. Second, although there were 13 major Indian languages, English was widely used in commerce and education. The existence of industries was also a draw. While the developing economy was based on agriculture, a wide spectrum of industries was in existence, breaking ground for future industrialization. Finally, and most important for us, was the matter of education. Literacy rates in India were climbing at unprecedented rates. The number of graduates and postgraduates in the country would be 9 million by 1985, with 39 million undergraduate students enrolled in universities and colleges throughout the country. India had 150 universities, more than 6,000 colleges, and 100 social science research institutes. All of these educational institutions fostered a demand for the products we could provide.

Cross-Cultural Challenges

However, despite so many factors in favor of India, there were a host of cross-cultural challenges to doing business in the country. First of all, the relationship between India and the United States in the mid-1970s was strained. Perceptions of India carried by mass media in the United States portrayed the country as riddled with poverty, hunger, and disease, and such depictions cast doubt on the feasibility of developing a market in India. Moreover, relatively few American firms that were operating in India gained respect from the Indians. American publishing firms had long used India as a market for their out-of-circulation textbooks. American political and economic opportunism elicited distrust on the part of Indian nationals, and political relations between the two countries were strained. Americans also distrusted the business environment, which insisted on local majority ownership and was heavily encumbered by bureaucratic red tape.

The primary concern for George and me, as we considered a move into India, was the relationship between the United States and India. In geopolitical terms, India was seen as favoring Russia (called the USSR in those days), and the United States was perceived as favoring Pakistan. The relationship between the United States and India was further strained in 1971 when India signed a friendship treaty with Russia designed to allow the exchange of Indian consumer goods for Russian oil and weapons. According to some Indian nationals, as India developed further ties with Russia, American firms operating in India lost the respect of Indian nationals, and an attitude of distrust encumbered dealings between Indian and American firms.

Another consideration we could not overlook was the stability of the country's currency. The value of the Indian rupee was falling at a rate of 10% a year. If we failed to consider what their exposure would be to further or more rapid devaluation of the rupee, the escalated devaluation of foreign currency could spell potential disaster for SAGE Publications in India.

One additional challenge that had historically deterred Americans from establishing joint ventures in India was government bureaucracy. The Indian bureaucracy was all-pervasive, and strictly enforced rules governed every aspect of industry in India. This was complicated by the Indian government having developed an environment hostile to foreign investment. The country feared that the flow of money from outside investors would lead to foreign control of the Indian economy and perhaps the culture as well. They were also afraid of an outflow of dividends and an inflow of foreign equipment that might inhibit the growth of Indian industries.

The Indian government kept strict control over all aspects of business, including expansion, automation, capital imports, and how to raise capital. To enforce this control, government personnel were posted in all plants to ensure that duties were paid on every invoice. If the company neglected to pay duty on even one invoice, government personnel had the authority to shut down the entire plant. The threat of shutdown was of greater concern to multinational companies than locally owned companies, because multinational companies were often bound by home office rules that prohibited the use of bribes in business dealings.

Indian companies avoided paying taxes by not reporting many transactions to the government. When government personnel detected such transactions, the Indian firm would respond by offering "black money," a bribe, to the government official. Indian nationals, as well as Americans doing business in India, noted that the existence of this underground economy accomplished everything from speeding up telephone installation to saving a company thousands of dollars in excise taxes.

Governmental regulation was perhaps most apparent in the area of personnel management. Once operations were established, laws governed personnel working hours and holidays. Office workers typically were restricted to 40 hours of work a week. Companies were required to provide 18 holidays, 3 to 4 weeks of vacation, 1 to 2 weeks of casual leave, and 2 weeks of sick leave to every employee. In total, this meant 9 to 11 weeks of paid leave annually for each employee.

The Indian government was also heavily involved in the retention of employees. Hiring an employee in India needed to be very carefully considered, as Indian regulations made firing an employee impossible unless there was proof of theft or assault. The process of dismissal could easily take a year, during which time the employee maintained at least 75% of his or her salary paid by the company.

Additional Challenges

As business grew, we knew we would face additional challenges unique to doing business in a developing country. Publishing was not an established industry in India. There were numerous publishing companies, but most had a different conception of what it took to publish a journal or book. This meant that we would be unable to hire experienced editors away from other publishers. Instead, we would have to look for individuals with master's degrees in journalism or related fields, then train them in the techniques, craft, and business of publishing.

George and I recognized the impact that understanding and working within Indian traditions and customs would have on our success. For instance, machines were prohibitively expensive due to Indian import taxes. In California, computers were critical to the publishing process. Books and journals were edited online. Mailing lists and order processing were also computerized. This computer-based technology that kept us operating smoothly in California could not be used in India. Instead, the structure of SAGE Publications in India would be labor-intensive.

Verbal communication was another key area requiring cultural sensitivity. Many differences showed up in simple conversations. Shaking one's head side to side signified agreement in most parts of India and disagreement in the United States. Other aspects of verbal communication varied between the two cultures as well. Formal names were very important in India. Until an Indian suggested that his first name be used, his formal name should be used. Communication with women was vastly different between the two cultures. Few women were in management positions in India. Women's roles were generally confined to the home. This cultural norm affected business, because Indian men often would not listen to a woman in a business meeting.

Nonverbal communication could be problematic as well. Indians do not shrug their shoulders to communicate "I don't know." They raise the palm of their right hand toward the ceiling and twist the hand from side to side. Acceptable physical distance when carrying on a conversation also had to be considered. George and I tried to keep a respectful distance from Indians, thereby allowing for their private space. In greeting Indian natives, we learned the importance of not reaching out to shake the hand of an Indian. Instead, we learned to touch our own palms together and raise them slightly in the form of a welcome.

Optimism Prevails

George and I believed that the cross-cultural issues could be overcome. Our optimism was due to us having placed ourselves, in the 16 years SAGE Publications had been in business, among the top social science publishers. We had become recognized as a source of critical information in fields as diverse as communications, research methodology, government, criminology, and family issues. We had been selective, had achieved greater presence, and had provided higher quality than our competitors in the United States.

In our niche, the competitive market for SAGE Publications in India held promise. The only other competitor in the Indian social science publication market at the time was Oxford University Press (OUP). Oxford's publishing program in academic fields was high priced and failed to explore emerging trends, focusing instead on the large profitable dictionary and school textbook business. It was not unusual for OUP to take up to two years to decide whether to publish a book.

We believed that the mail-order business we had developed in the United States would transfer relatively easily into the Indian market. In India, specialized retail outlets did not exist. There were only 25 to 30 broadly stocked bookstores in the entire country. Additionally, the 700 million Indian citizens were spread out over a huge subcontinent with huge divides between the urban "haves" and the rural poor. No other publishing houses were using a direct mail marketing technique to reach the Indian market. Given our expertise in direct marketing, the lack of retail outlets, the widely dispersed population, and the fact that no one else was taking this approach to marketing books and journals in India, direct mail appeared to offer significant competitive advantage to our entrance into India.

Further support for using direct mail marketing came from the availability of free mailing lists. The secretary general of the Indian Social Science Research Council promised to provide us with a newly compiled directory if

Sara at Yearbook Office,
Queens College, City University
of New York, spring 1961.

Sara at Pergamon's Annual Holiday Ball,
Oxford Town Hall, December 1963.

Our Gang, Oxford, c. 1963-64. Back row, Sara in red sari, Loni (now Loni Sinha) in pink sari, Manu (now Manu Roy Chakravartty) in print sari with maroon sweater. All young men were doing second degrees at one of the Oxford Colleges and thus have various degrees from Oxford University. The front row includes Sunil ("Sunny") Sinha, currently on the physics faculty of University of California, San Diego (wearing eyeglasses), and Bimal Jalan, who has served (among other positions) as Chief Economic Advisor to the Prime Minister of India (Indira Gandhi) and Chairman of the Reserve Bank of India. The photographer is Gautham Chakravartty, who has since had a distinguished career in international banking.

Sara and George, meeting Sara's mother at LAX Airport, 1967.

London, 1970s.
Katy's dog.
Dillon's Book Shop.

Rose Miller and David
McCune, late 1980s.

Daryab Singh and the SAGE India company
car (Hindustan Motors), India, early 1980s.
Mr. Singh is still the company driver and has
been employed by SAGE India for 28 years.

Early 1980s, Tejeshwar Singh and wife Brinda
(with Sara on the left and George on the right).

Sara, George, Rose Miller,
and Marian Jackson at
the London flat, 1986.

George McCune,
May 1990.

Daniel Thursz served as a member
of SAGE's Board of Directors for
more than two decades. He was a
former Dean of the School of Social
Work at the University of Maryland,
a SAGE author and series editor,
and a founding member of the
McCune Foundation's Board.

Margaret Sirot, 1995.

Professor Peter Lyman, who served as a SAGE Inc.
Board Member for more than a decade, until his
death in 2008, and his wife, Professor Barrie Thorne,
University of California, Berkeley, enjoying a break
for tea after a lengthy Board meeting in London.

David McCune and Blaise Simqu in the early 1990s in one of many congratulatory moments for a successful journal acquisition.

Sara at Ikarum, Nigeria, one of her two "Millennium Villages," 2006.

SAGE's offices in Delhi
since late 2006.

"Learning Has No Borders":
Asia-Pacific Opening Ceremonies
in Singapore, 2007 (Tejeshwar
Singh and Stephen Barr).

Sara and Duke, 2009.

Barbara Hake, receptionist at the Thousand Oaks office, has been greeting visitors for more than 20 years.

Top row, left to right:
Michael Quinn Patton,
David Goldfield, Melvin
Oliver, Gareth Morgan

Bottom row, left to right:
Ellen Wartella, Sara,
Molefi Kete Asante

Photo taken at the
45th anniversary event
in Santa Barbara, 2010.

Stephen Barr speaking at the opening ceremonies
for SAGE Asia-Pacific in Singapore, 2007.

The SAGE Asia-Pacific
offices, Singapore, 2007.

Stephen Barr speaking at
the launch of the Tejeshwar
Singh Memorial Fellowships
in Delhi, 2008.

Professor T. N. Madan
speaking at the launch of the
Tejeshwar Singh Memorial
Fellowships in Delhi, 2008.

Poster of Tejeshwar Singh at the February 2008 World Book
Fair, New Delhi, India, shortly after his death in December 2007.

Kim Lyman, Manager for Organizational Development,
conducting one of the many ongoing training sessions
offered through Human Resources (2010).

Vivek Mehra speaking in Delhi (February 2009) to honor
the memory of Tejeshwar Singh, Founding Managing
Director of SAGE India from 1981 to 2006, and to announce
the setting up of two fellowships in his memory.

At executive meetings, collegial discussions are held and
decisions affecting the future of the company are made.
From left to right: Blaise Simqu, Ziyad Marar, Jayne Marks,
Tracey Ozmina, Chris Hickok, and Leigh Peake (2010).

Librarians who attended the SAGE/Thomson ISI event at Tsinghua University, Beijing, in 2009. In the back row (from left) are Rosalia Garcia, Director of Journals Sales, SAGE Asia-Pacific; Dr. Wei Ping Yue, Thomson Reuters; Blaise Simqu; Steve Golden; Stephen Barr; and Nicola Everitt, Director of Book Sales, SAGE Asia-Pacific.

Sara's visit to the Delhi head office of SAGE India in 2009 (left to right: Kate Wilde, Vivek Mehra, Sara, Stephen Barr, and Judi Weisbart).

India office staff listening to one of Vivek Mehra's regular monthly company meetings (2009). On this occasion, Steve Golden and Stephen Barr were both present and spoke at the company meeting also.

Sara in Delhi in February 2009 to announce the creation of a Tejeshwar Singh Memorial Fellowship in the Social Sciences.

we entered the Indian market. This directory mailing list contained the names and addresses of 8,000 social scientists pursuing research, which paralleled SAGE's business focus.

The respect and attention SAGE bestowed upon authors would benefit our mission in India, even though relationships with Indian authors would need to be tailored to account for cultural differences. Tejeshwar Singh, a publisher with more than 20 years of experience in India (who eventually became our partner), related a story that highlighted the differences in dealing with Indian scholars. He told of the time early in his career when he had gotten friendly with a scholar, and the two had entered into a discussion along with another scholar. During the discussion, Tejeshwar interjected his opinions on a certain book. Later, Tejeshwar attempted to obtain a contract for a book from the scholar but was flatly refused. The scholar had taken offense at Tejeshwar's expressing his opinions. In India, publishers do not have the stature of academics!

One segment of the SAGE market virtually untouched in India was the journal market. Very few journals existed in India. Those journals that did exist were produced by universities or institutions with in-house editors. Unlike their Western equivalents, the Indian journals did not use peer reviews. Most journals were running three years behind schedule. SAGE in India would have difficulty establishing reasonable subscription rates. Subscribers were paying 70 rupees (less than $10) for an annual subscription of two editions of 500 pages each at the time. With such low subscription rates, we could not compete on price.

If we were to move into journal production, however, SAGE Publications in India could bring numerous benefits to the journal business that would justify higher subscription rates. As in the United States, SAGE in India would institute peer reviews for all the journals they published, thereby enhancing the caliber of articles that were published. Journals would be produced in a timely manner. These journals would be free of errors, with professional quality desk editing (all by hand because computers were not widely used in India at the time).

A Decision Is Made

Given that the competitive climate seemed right for a move into India, George and I contemplated the various forms a move into India could take.

After a certain amount of to-and-fro correspondence and phone calls, we arranged to visit India again approximately 15 months later, in May 1981.

Once in India, we met with the highly regarded Macmillan India Vice President, Tejeshwar Singh. During the conversation, Tejeshwar found he and George had much more to talk about than a possible arrangement between two organizations. Tejeshwar described that initial meeting as "a meeting of the minds." This positive interaction with Tejeshwar led George and me to consider the possibility of entering into a joint-venture arrangement with Tejeshwar.

Over the years, Tejeshwar had developed an impressive résumé. He had graduated from Oxford University with a politics, philosophy, and economics degree. After his return to India, Tejeshwar became somewhat of a celebrity when he was selected to read national news on Indian television. Tejeshwar had accrued more than 10 years of publishing experience. The most recent 8 years had been spent with Macmillan India, a branch of Macmillan UK. Having started as an editor, Tejeshwar had worked his way up to become vice president in charge of the Delhi sales region.

A joint-venture agreement with Tejeshwar offered us numerous opportunities, including allowing us to establish a direct marketing campaign in India designed to target the type of customers we wanted to reach. Working with an Indian native such as Tejeshwar would give us an edge when dealing with the Indian bureaucracy. However, this type of joint venture would require that George and I sacrifice a significant portion of any profits we stood to earn in India, as well as requiring a significant capital outlay to establish the business. Also, there was an issue of control. With George and I working out of the United States, and the joint-venture partner located in India, the Indian partner would be responsible for carrying out the SAGE vision in India.

We took Tejeshwar to stay on a houseboat in Kashmir and spent hours every day for a week working out a *Memorandum of Understanding* for our venture. Tejeshwar went back to Delhi to set the lawyers and accountants to work and, of course, to organize an announcement party for our closest authors and advisers. We returned to Delhi in time to host the party at the Sheraton Maurya Hotel (still a favorite watering hole and home to one of my absolutely top picks on the Delhi restaurant scene for North Indian cuisine). It was a great time, and we knew we had a lot to do, but we were most definitely on our way!

SAGE India was launched as a jointly owned company with the majority of its shares (60%) owned by Tejeshwar Singh, in line with Indian law at the time, which required that Indian companies have majority Indian ownership. Of the remaining shares, 24% were owned by SAGE California and 16% by George and me.

The new company had a trading agreement with SAGE California, which governed its right to use the SAGE name as well as the terms on which it was able to distribute in India the books and journals published by SAGE worldwide. The ownership remained on this basis until Tejeshwar's retirement from the role of Managing Director, at which point his shares were purchased by SAGE (Indian law having changed in the interim to allow a foreign company to have complete ownership of an Indian subsidiary).

Report in the 1990s

During the early years of SAGE in India, George and I went over on average once a year, and then our visits slowed to every other year, as the business became more established. My trip in late December 1993 and early January of 1994 gave me an opportunity to see the growth and expansion of SAGE India, which had a banner year in 1993, just as SAGE, Inc. and SAGE, Ltd had. It was also fun to see old friends on the staff and to visit with a few new faces who had joined in the past year to help SAGE India continue to grow in 1994 and beyond.

In addition to my visit to SAGE's central offices in New Delhi, I visited SAGE India's Calcutta sales office for the first time, which was quite an experience. It was good to see the office bustle with preparation for the annual Calcutta Book Fair. Preparations were also afoot for the biannual World Book Fair in Delhi, which would provide SAGE India with an early boost to record sales in 1994, as well as a busy start to the new year.

In the mid-1990s, publishing companies in India, as with most businesses in India at that time, were benefiting from an improved economic climate. This was evident in the country's currency stability, good economic growth, and relative political stability. Reflecting these upturns, SAGE India's growth rate in 1993 exceeded 20% over 1992 in sales and would do so again in 1994.

For the first time, SAGE India's yearly sales had exceeded 10 million rupees (more than $330,000). The company was profitable, and foreign remittances to SAGE, Inc. and SAGE, Ltd were strong and steady.

One difficulty that SAGE India experienced, as did most Indian publishers who had affiliated with American or British firms, was that the cost of importing publications in rupees was often prohibitive, so the number of copies of imported books or subscriptions that could be sold in India was severely limited.

For example, an Indian-originated journal might have sold for 500 rupees per annual subscription, whereas an American-originated title was likely to sell for 3,900 rupees per annum. Books originating in the United States typically sold for more than 1,200 rupees (in the hardcover editions), whereas a similar title published by SAGE in New Delhi might carry a hardcover price of 225 rupees.

So it was not surprising that much of SAGE India's growth had come from a surge in sales of locally published titles—including some very successful books in management and organization studies, such as *Young Managers at the Crossroads* and *Managerial Transformation by Values*. SAGE India also launched four new journals in 1994, a move that increased their list of locally published periodicals by 50% in one year! Other initiatives for 1994 included the broadening of job descriptions and responsibilities for SAGE India's middle-management team (along with a lot of in-house management training and development).

VKRV Rao and Gandhi

On one visit, early in SAGE India's history, Tejeshwar accompanied George and me on a trip to Bangalore, a major city and home to some of the most well-recognized colleges and research institutions in India (known today as the Silicon Valley of India, because of its position as the nation's leading IT exporter). We met with VKRV Rao, who had been SAGE India's first book author in 1982. At the time, he was already an elderly gentleman, and he had been the chief economic adviser to India's Prime Minister Indira Gandhi during her first terms. In his retirement, he was doing some very important research at the University of Bangalore.

We arranged to meet Rao at the hotel (the same one where the movie *A Passage to India* was filmed), but George became ill and so stayed in our room while Tejeshwar and I met with Professor Rao for what turned out to be a very memorable lunch. As we were eating, I looked across the table and thought that Rao had to be of the generation that crossed paths with Mahatma Gandhi, and so on the spur of the moment, I asked him if he had known the great leader. Rao replied yes, mentioning that he'd worked for Gandhi, his face lighting up as he spoke, and he reminisced for a good 20 minutes about Gandhi's humanity, his temperament, and his vision.

Rao had been much younger then, some 30 years earlier, but was already a distinguished economist and academic at the time. (In England and in India, as one of the many "outposts of the empire," a person could be what the British call *seconded,* allowed to go back and forth between being a policy adviser and an academic without taking a giant cut in pay or a change in status, since both areas were respected and legitimate.) That 20 minutes, in which the usually vocal Tejeshwar, who was then a part-time television news announcer, didn't say a word, was very precious to me.

Millennium Update

On December 15, 2007, Tejeshwar Singh suffered a heart attack and passed away. While he'd played a major role in Indian media (his rich, perfectly accented diction was regarded as the epitome of correct spoken English, used in school classes around India to teach pronunciation), including appearances on TV and in a number of Indian films, Tejeshwar had devoted his life to work in publishing. He was the founding Managing Director of the new SAGE India in 1981 and, over the next 25 years, grew that business into a highly successful and influential Indian publishing company, which became one of the premier publishers in South Asia. In 2006, he moved on from the role of Managing Director to become the Chairman of the Board of SAGE India. Throughout this time, he was recognized as one of the major authorities in the Indian publishing industry, frequently quoted in the national press on publishing issues. He was internationally known as a representative of publishing in the developing world and participated in panels run by UNESCO and other agencies on issues of international flows of information.

Even more important to Tejeshwar than his media and publishing career was his family life. He was a devoted family man who is survived by his wife, Brinda, his daughters, Aamana and Sonali, and his parents, Gurbachan and Shamma Singh. He will be remembered by his many colleagues and contacts worldwide for his exceptional personal qualities: his gift for friendship, his personal warmth, and his zest for life. He had tremendous charisma combined with a generosity of spirit that set him apart.

A Personal Tribute to Tejeshwar Singh

I feel that I have been personally very fortunate in my colleagues over the years, because no one builds an organization alone, and I have had some truly remarkable partners. Tejeshwar Singh was one of these. Tejeshwar was not just a person who meshed with George and me in a business sense, but he also was in sync with our goals, dreams, and vision. In addition, Tejeshwar (we nicknamed him "TJ") was someone who shared—and will, in my memory, always share—our values on both a personal and a professional level. This sense of shared values made for a rare relationship and friendship in doing business together, and Tejeshwar was a truly rare human being.

It was extraordinary to work with Tejeshwar, to be on the phone with him once we succeeded in establishing a regular pattern of phone calls (despite the 13½-hour time difference), to meet with him, whether in California or London or New Delhi, and to travel with him (and often with his immediate family) in various parts of India. Because he was a regular news reader (in English, on India's national TV evening news program), traveling with Tejeshwar in India was the equivalent of traveling with Dan Rather in the United States. George and I were always both amused and astounded in our travels with him, and the people that he introduced us to demonstrated not only his rapport with authors and editors but also the breadth and depth of his intellect and his extraordinary ability to communicate.

Tejeshwar had what I can only describe as something more than what people talk about when they refer to charisma. It shone out from him like a beacon, and it stays in one's heart and mind. It always will. Tejeshwar was a very special person and a very special colleague, a very special human being, a very special husband, father, son, brother, a member of his extended family, a member of my extended family, and a member of SAGE's global family. I know that George felt this way during the last decade of his life as we worked together to build and extend that global family. I will always feel especially blessed by that memory, and I believe that everyone who ever met Tejeshwar Singh feels exactly the same way.

SAGE India Today

At the time of Tejeshwar's untimely death, we had a Managing Director, Vivek Mehra, in place and prepared for the transition. Vivek is doing a terrific job with his India management team and is a part of the SAGE International management team that meets twice a year. Going through Stephen Barr or personally, the team reports to SAGE, Inc.'s and SAGE, Ltd's Board of Directors and shareholders and have each played an incredible role in SAGE's growth. (For more about the international growth of SAGE, see Chapter 11.)

CHAPTER 9

SAGE London Takes Off

By 1981, a decade after opening our London office, SAGE Publications, Inc. was established and growing in the United States, Canada, the UK, and Europe. We also had active distribution partners in East Asia, Australia, and New Zealand (via California), and SAGE London was actively forging ahead into the Middle East and Africa.

But then, some serious difficulties and challenges arose. In 1982, George had open-heart surgery at Cedars Sinai Hospital in Los Angeles. While he was recovering, we invited David Brooks to come over and help run the American business. He liked California and wanted to be closer to his son, who was by then living in Connecticut, and also knew a lot about the company, so we offered him the job of President and he accepted. But the financial times were tough, it being the middle of one of Reagan's deepest recessions, and David soon decided to return to the UK. By then, George was recovered enough to become President of SAGE, Inc., and I took the roles of Chairman and Publisher.

Meanwhile, Back in London . . .

We needed a new Managing Director to replace David Brooks, who did not return to his position. Matt Jackson helped us in the recruitment of Brooks's replacement, David Hill, who'd been the Editorial Director at SAGE, Ltd. We had hired Hill in 1983 along with Farrell Burnett (David concentrated on politics and sociology and Farrell focused on communications and psychology), and together they had built a publishing program to parallel the established programs of SAGE in California. Hill and I were good friends, so we decided to promote him to Managing Director in 1988. It turned out to be a wise choice. As Managing Director, David Hill relaunched SAGE, Ltd's books and journals program and built us into a major publishing house "across the pond."

David Hill had been born into a publishing family. His father, Alan Hill, was a well-known publisher who built Heinemann, Ltd, a publisher of educational books, where David also had had a successful career; his brother, Stephen Hill, was and still is a very distinguished sociologist at the University of London. David was obviously well networked in the industry, which would be of immense benefit to us, particularly in the early days of electronic transmissions.

David Hill joined SAGE, Ltd on condition that he be given a shareholding in the company. George and I were reluctant to dilute our shareholding to accommodate his terms, but his publishing record greatly impressed us, and we wanted to hire him. Matt Jackson was certain that David would build us into a publisher of first choice in our fields, so in order to break the deadlock between us and David on the share position, he volunteered to sell David ten of his own shares, which was 20% of his holding, and David accepted.

Meanwhile, David Brooks, at the time the outgoing Managing Director of SAGE, Ltd, was required by his contract to sell all his shares in SAGE, Ltd before leaving. This meant that a valuation of those shares had to be arrived at, since they had never been valued before. We needed a formula that at any time would calculate the value of SAGE, Ltd shares (so that it wouldn't be left to an individual or a committee to decide). Together with Matt, we drew up the formula, which would be used in the future to include not only the actual turnover of the company as a calculating point but also the profitability.

David Hill turned out to be a very effective publisher and Managing Director, and by the time Matt Jackson sold his remaining shares in 1997, their value was much higher than anyone could reasonably have forecast 25 years previously.

Matt Jackson recruited several members of the Board and of the marketing and production division who are still there after many successful years with the company. All of them are greatly valued not only by SAGE, Ltd and SAGE, Inc. but also by our competitors. All of them at some time or another have been the targets of headhunters acting for other companies. That they have remained with SAGE, we are convinced, is not only because we pay them the money that they are undoubtedly worth but also because for many of them, their first opportunity in publishing came with SAGE, Ltd, and they have a sense of gratitude and loyalty to the company as a result.

In 2001, Matt ceased to be a member of the Board of Directors of SAGE, Ltd and continued to act as a consultant to the Managing Director, currently Stephen Barr, and as appropriate to the shareholders, but no longer in his capacity as a non-executive director.

New Leadership: Stephen Barr

David Hill left SAGE, Ltd in 1996, replaced by Stephen Barr, who came to us originally from Open University. Stephen was at first our Sociology Editor in 1986 and then worked his way up to Editorial Director in 1988; from there, we promoted him to Managing Director in 1996. Stephen met his wife, Susan Worsey, at SAGE when she was the Counseling Psychology Editor, and today they have four children. Their youngest boy is in a private school, where Stephen drops him off every day before coming into the office. Susan has since gotten her teacher's certificate and is a schoolteacher, a job she loves, and I must say that she is even prettier today than when they first got married!

In a recent interview, Stephen talked of his early association with SAGE London and how he saw the company grow during the 1980s, the 1990s, and into the new millennium. I will let his words tell the story.

Reflections: Stephen Barr

A Decade of Expansion

When I came on board at SAGE in 1986, one of my earliest initiatives was publishing textbooks in collaboration with the Open University (OU). The OU was an early and innovative distance learning institution in the UK set up by then Prime Minister Harold Wilson in the 1960s to teach people through the medium of TV. It delivered lecture courses provided by the BBC, combined with print materials and seminars to provide an infrastructure for people to have classes in their local town.

The OU had a program for involving publishers in packaging parts of its content, which met a need both within the OU and outside. The publisher's job was to build book sales to the outside market, which would generate royalty income for the OU and make the books more cost-effective for the OU to publish. This arrangement turned out to be a good opportunity for SAGE, because the OU was willing to work with a newer publisher like SAGE; they wanted good marketing and sales at a very economical price, and SAGE could deliver on that.

The first proposal I put forward when I joined SAGE was an OU book. I had worked for OU before I came to SAGE, and I knew their system, so I had an insider advantage. In 1986, I bid for and we won many OU text-books, creating a program of co-publishing with OU that contributed to building our presence as a textbook publisher in the UK—a very signifi-cant development.

Even more significant, over the late 1980s, I would see a time of initial expansion for SAGE London in areas of research methods, sociology, communications/media studies, and counseling psychology.

Research Methods Expansion

In the late 1980s, the research methods publishing program was already a very strong program in California, and we knew there was a market for it in London, because we were selling the California books. Key developments in our expansion in research methods involved two authors—David Silverman and Stuart Clegg.

David Silverman, an eminent sociologist whose book *Communication and Medical Practice* we published in 1987, was the first author in our pub-lishing program of books on qualitative research, which have since been extremely successful. David's book demonstrated we could find equivalent authors in the UK and Europe that would sell in large quantities—not only in the UK/Europe market but also back in the United States. Silverman's research methods publishing with SAGE includes *The Politics of Field Research,* 1989 (co-edited by Jaber Gubrium); *Interpreting Qualitative Data,* 1993 (first edition sold over 20,000 copies); *Qualitative Research,* 1997; and *Doing Qualitative Research,* 1999 (sales to date over 37,000 copies). (Two other titles worth mentioning from the early days of the SAGE London research methods program are Nigel Fielding and Ray Lee's book, *Using Computers in Qualitative Research,* 1991, and Nigel Gilbert's *Researching Social Life,* 1992, the first edition of which sold over 25,000 copies.)

Stuart Clegg was another major author to come on board in the late 1980s. Clegg's first book with us, *Frameworks of Power,* was on a central sociology topic and was a serious, high-level book that did a lot to establish SAGE's credentials as a major UK/European publisher. Subsequently, the series of books he did with us have been in the domain of management and organization studies. Again, his work there has done a lot to frame SAGE London as a major player in organization studies. One of his subsequent books with SAGE was the *Handbook of Organization Studies,* published in 1996, which was the first real handbook published from SAGE London. It was a highly successful book and demonstrated we could develop major reference titles out of London that would sell internationally as well as in the U.S. market. The *Handbook of Organization Studies* was awarded the annual prize of the U.S. Academy of Management. Clegg's later textbook, *Managing and Organizations* (first edition 2004), has sold over 20,000 copies.

Expansion in Sociology

An important initiative during the 1980s was the signing of the *Theory, Culture & Society* series and the impact that acquisition had on SAGE and its growth. The context was a major philosophical shift going on in the academic environment within some of the key disciplines we were addressing in the late 1980s and early 1990s, known as the "cultural turn." Basically, a whole raft of disciplines started paying much more attention to the importance of culture than they previously had. This cultural turn was much wider than the field of sociology, affecting the social sciences and humanities more broadly.

There were two strong influences bringing this shift about in the late 1980s. One was the different world we were living in. Sociology as a discipline had developed in an environment where people's lives were mainly determined by issues such as work and class. Now we were in an environment where our lives seemed much more determined by factors such as our spending patterns, consumption, leisure, and other emerging trends. Our modern society tended to behave in different ways and have different rules than the society sociologists had been focused on originally.

A second driver of this shift was how European philosophy and social theory, represented by figures like Derrida, Foucault, and Baudrillard, was changing the way researchers thought about their subjects. The term *postmodernism* was ushered in by the cultural turn, raising questions of how modern society and culture were changing and becoming something new, something postmodern.

The journal *Theory, Culture & Society* (*TCS*), signed by SAGE London, was a place where those kinds of issues could be explored and discussed in an early form. The journal had been launched as a self-published journal in 1983, and very quickly every publisher who published journals wanted to sign it. SAGE won the bid, and we started publishing *TCS* in 1987.

Alongside the journal, in 1990 we started developing a *Theory, Culture & Society* book series. Books in this series had a huge impact on the perception of SAGE as a major publisher in the UK. Until that time, SAGE was perceived in the UK and in Europe mainly through our role as a distributer of books from the U.S. market. But the arrival of the *TCS* series was one of the major events that put us on the map. In sociology and in communications/media studies, it positioned SAGE as addressing the wave of new thinking that was going on, which positively reinforced SAGE's centrality as the publisher for those key disciplines.

The *TCS* series launch included titles of a high standard with authors such as Pierre Bourdieu, Mike Featherstone, Bryan Turner, and John Urry. Subsequent books in the series included works by Scott Lash, Ulrich Beck, and Jean Baudrillard, to mention only a few. The original books in the series sold well, with many of them selling more than 10,000 copies. The series went on to publish a number of other high-selling titles and is now a series of over 100 books—a substantial enterprise!

Communication/Media Studies—European Style

Because cultural studies tend to overlap with communication/media studies, many scholars within the communications discipline were strongly influenced by the cultural turn and the kinds of issues that were being explored in the *TCS* series. At the time, we already had a position in publishing good European work in communication studies—one of our early books was a classic textbook by Denis McQuail, *Mass Communication Theory.* But publishing the *TCS* series positioned us at the forefront of the communication field.

In the United States, the discipline called communication studies brings together the study of the media with other forms of communication, such as interpersonal communication and communication in organizations. In Europe, however, communication isn't taught in an integrated communication department, but rather the interpersonal aspects are taught in social psychology, and the media studies aspects are taught either within a communication department or as part of a wider social science program.

As we built a publishing program focused on the European brand of communication studies, it inevitably meant having a strong program in what we think of in Europe as media studies. This program was similar to what was going on in the United States under the label of communication studies, not a complete departure, with the most distinctive difference being the impact of the cultural turn—the shift in thinking. The different emphasis of the list out of SAGE London actually helped SAGE in the United States establish a stronger presence in this end of the discipline.

By building a parallel program to the U.S. communications list, we were deepening our presence in two domains. One was in media studies in the UK and Europe, and the other was in the area of discursive psychology, which was a European/UK parallel of the interpersonal communication work going on in the United States. There are now three journals on our list for this subfield: *Discourse & Society, Discourse & Communication,* and *Discourse Studies.*

We also developed a number of journals addressing other issues within the cultural turn in different disciplines. For example, the journal *Organization* represented new thinking in management and organization studies, and *Culture & Psychology* was launched to address a range of issues relating to culture from a psychological perspective.

Expansion in Counseling Psychology

Another significant innovation in the early stages of the publishing program in the 1980s was in counseling psychology. Counseling was becoming more strongly established as a field in the UK, and Farrell Burnett, who was the Acquisition Editor for psychology up until 1988, had identified counseling as a potentially significant area.

Farrell worked with Windy Dryden (who had already published a major textbook on counseling, *Handbook of Individual Therapy,* that SAGE was subsequently able to acquire) on a series that would tackle each of the major approaches to counseling, called *Counselling in Action.* Since its launch 20 years ago, there have been nearly 20 titles (some of which have been SAGE's best sellers) to define SAGE's position in counseling. It was the first British series in counseling, and most of the books are still in print, being used in most counseling training courses in the UK. Dryden's first book in the series was *Key Issues for Counselling in Action* (co-edited by Andrew Reeves in its second edition), which sold tremendously well.

Farrell left SAGE before the *Counselling in Action* series came out, but alongside the counseling list, she was also building a core psychology publishing program. One of the best early books she commissioned in that program was *Discourse and Social Psychology* by Jonathan Potter and Margaret Wetherell. That book similarly set SAGE as an innovative player in the new movements in psychology, and we subsequently built a strong publishing program on the back of having established ourselves with these early works.

A subsequent series of independent books in counseling commissioned by my wife, Susan Worsey, among other series (*Key Figures in Counselling and Psychotherapy* and *Counselling in Practice*), further expanded our psychology list and built SAGE London into being a premier publisher in the UK.

By the end of the 1980s, we had mapped out an entire domain of areas for SAGE London that paralleled the lists and disciplines already developed in the United States. Much of our development since then has been in deepening and strengthening our presence in disciplines that we entered into during the mid- to late 1980s.

Growth of Journals List in the 1990s

The 1990s were very exciting times at SAGE London, in terms of building a program of new journal publishing—a development also unfolding "across the pond" in the California offices. The key journal for getting that program moving was *Discourse & Society,* launched in 1990. *Discourse & Society* was a tremendous success, and again it was a contribution to building our presence and strength in communications studies. On the back of that success, we launched over 30 journals during the 1990s, adding 20 more by 2004. By then, we had a team of people working in the London office: Karen Phillips in sociology publishing, Ziyad Marar in psychology, Sue Jones in management and organizational studies, Susan Worsey in counseling, and David Hill continuing to do political science while being Managing Director.

Ziyad Marar joined SAGE London in the Journals Marketing Department in July 1989, where he was involved in the early stages of the journal launches we undertook during the 1990s. In 1992, Ziyad was appointed Psychology and Politics Editor but worked predominantly in expanding our psychology list. Today, he is Deputy Managing Director and Publishing Director, managing editorial, sales and marketing, and the production department. He is one of two Deputy Managing Directors in the London office; Katharine Jackson is the other, managing human resources, distribution, and finance.

We will let Ziyad tell the story of his contribution to the expansion of SAGE London in building our psychology program and our journal list.

Reflections: Ziyad Marar

Growing Psychology

I became the Psychology Editor in 1992, but even before that time, when I was in journals marketing, I had an influence on the psychology list, launching ground-breaking journals such as *Theory & Psychology* and *Feminism & Psychology.* In 1992, the focus was on social psychology, a subfield of psychology, and an even smaller subfield known as "critical" social psychology.

Critical social psychology tended toward a political edge and was theoretically innovative. While a vibrant part of our list, it was a fairly narrow part of the greater field of psychology, and we needed to branch out.

As Psychology Editor, I set about to broaden our psychology program to take in more traditional areas. It was also my intention to protect and preserve that narrow and vibrant strand of critical social psychology, because it had served us well and it tied to other parts of our publishing of work influenced by the cultural turn that Stephen Barr has already mentioned.

One way of broadening the list was to take on publishing research methods within psychology, both qualitative and quantitative. Examples of this include the first edition of Andy Field's *Discovering Statistics Using SPSS* (now SAGE London's best selling title of all time) and Glynis M. Breakwell's *Research Methods in Psychology,* now in its third edition. Another key area was in mainstream social psychology, as exemplified by launching the journal *Group Processes and Intergroup Relations,* which led to our publishing a very significant social psychology series edited by Professor Mike Hogg that drew in major names in the field. Other departures in psychology included work in developmental and cognitive psychology.

Meanwhile, the critical tradition of social psychology we had so strongly supported did not go neglected. There were many who contributed to it, such as Kenneth Gergen, Kurt Danziger, and Jonathan Potter, all of whom we were publishing during this time. Rom Harré, a professor of philosophy and psychology at both Oxford University and Georgetown University with the highest international profile, has written many books on the philosophy of science, as well as social and philosophical psychology, that have been extremely influential.

In the early 1990s, Rom's work was being published by Blackwell, among others, and I remember meeting him in 1993 when Sara, Stephen Barr, and I all went up to Oxford to persuade him to move to SAGE. It was a day on which Steve Barr got what we thought was food poisoning and went progressively greener during the lunch. (Sara recalled that it turned out to be a virulent strain of influenza.) Meanwhile, Sara and I did a total pincer move on Rom, and he agreed to do not just one book but a whole package of books for us in 1994. The main book he published was called *The Discursive Mind,* and then he also co-edited a three-volume set of books, including *Rethinking Psychology* and *Rethinking Methods in Psychology.* We had five books from Rom in the end.

When I started, I not only focused on the critical psychology piece and the more mainstream program in psychology, but also balanced across books and journals, doing quite a lot of journal publishing in psychology. There are journals now being published in volumes 12 and 15 that I started—*Culture & Psychology, Journal of Health Psychology, Clinical Child Psychology and Psychiatry*—and in many other areas that are great successes today. I was also publishing across a range of handbooks and textbooks, as well as supplementary titles.

I left the psychology editor position to become Editorial Director when Stephen Barr was promoted to Managing Director, but I stayed directly involved in the psychology list for a good while. The time I was commissioning was actually a five- to six-year period, but the focus on psychology has been close to my heart throughout my time at SAGE (not least because it is also my academic background). Steve had previously been Editorial Director, and I replaced him, taking on the responsibility for all of our programs across a range of areas in which psychology was only one.

In 2006, I took on my present role as Deputy Managing Director and Publishing Director, a new role created because SAGE had grown so much at that point. When I first joined, back in 1986, there were approximately 40 people at the company in London, and now we have close to 300 there. In revenue terms, the growth has been equally as startling. I remember when I became Editorial Director in 2006, we had made our first £1 million net profits in London. During our most recent year, 2009, we delivered over £17 million, so the order of magnitude is substantial in terms of the financial impact and significance for SAGE Group. (For more about SAGE London's activities and growth into the first decade of the new millennium, see Chapter 11, pp. 139–142.)

A Celebration in Words: SAGE 1965–2005
Rom Harré, *Oxford University, England, and Georgetown University, Washington, D.C.*

My abiding recollections of working with Sara always involve a good meal. Papers, drafts, and proofs lie scattered about the table and even on the floor. The Four Seasons in Georgetown is one of Washington's "top spots" and of course just the place for a SAGE working breakfast.

Each book I have done with SAGE is associated with something similar. This was publishing in the old style. The publishing house was a place for business no doubt, but it was also an intellectual center, a place where ideas were forged, criticized, and brought to fruition. In such a place, friendships grew, and the product, the published book, has a different depth from a mere commodity.

A few years ago, my wife and I were returning to New Zealand for our golden wedding anniversary, passing through Los Angeles on that grueling journey to the South Pacific. "Let's get together while you are in L.A.," Sara had said. Well! Quite a get-together. At the airport, a limousine waited to take us to a splendid hotel looking out over a marina. After a pause for freshening up, we sat down to a memorable anniversary dinner.

This is how a great publishing house should be—warmly collegial and coolly business-like at the same time. It was Sara's great achievement to bring this about while other houses were becoming book factories. Happily, the same atmosphere is still evident in the new generation of editors with whom I have had the pleasure to work.

Stephen Barr now describes how we expanded by moving into science, technology, medicine (STM) publishing and made an early shift to online publishing, beginning in the 1990s.

Reflections: Stephen Barr

Other Developments of the 1990s

During the early 1990s, as the Internet and the World Wide Web developed, it became apparent that there was going to be a transformation of how publishing took place, and we realized we needed to move our journals from being static print objects to being electronic, at least alongside of the print. (As I recall, the company in California had acquired the same organizational learning, and basically both sides of the company were developing our online presence at about the same pace.)

In the early 1990s, SAGE London became involved in something called the Super Journal Project, a collaborative exercise by the major UK-based journal publishers to test out the models for setting up an electronic journal. Our participation meant that as the industry wrestled with issues of electronic delivery of journals, SAGE was fully involved in that learning process.

We started by doing experiments with online versions of some of our journals by 1997, and by 1999, we had rolled out that effort to all of our journals. Since then, we have faced some complicated issues that have arisen from the electronic delivery of journals, but having had our content available in electronic form from fairly early on, we were able to address those changes as we've needed to.

Another shift during the 1990s involved our expansion into new fields. SAGE was focused on the social sciences for the first 30 years of our existence, but as the publishing programs grew, we began to realize that if SAGE wanted to continue to grow vigorously, then it was going to become constraining to work only within the social sciences. By the late 1990s, David McCune, chief executive in the United States, had decided we should move into STM publishing. (See Chapter 10 for more details on this transition.)

The initial move, done out of the U.S. office, was the creation of an imprint called SAGE Science Press, a way of saying we were serious about doing STM publishing. Eventually, it was decided to take STM development on jointly, and so we specialized out of each office—California would develop health and medical publishing, and London would focus on engineering publishing, reflecting the strengths of people based in each office.

This division lasted until 2005, when we agreed, since there was such a huge potential in the health and medical area, that London would develop alongside of California in that area. We've now built a strong team that works on medical and health publishing in addition to our list in engineering.

Today, SAGE globally has more than 100 journals that are health and medical related, more than half of which are strictly medical and nursing, and this list is going up rapidly on both sides of the ocean. Within the UK, the main launch program is a journal series called *Therapeutic Advances,* with up to 15 titles—each one for a different medical specialty—by the time the series is completed.

Another way we expanded in the 1990s was by acquisitions. The major effort in that direction was the purchasing of an entire company in 1998 called Paul Chapman Publishing. Because Paul Chapman had two main publishing programs, one in social sciences (which overlapped with products SAGE London already had) and another in education, it was an incremental addition to our existing range of content. The education publishing program consisted of textbooks in education and related fields, such as developmental psychology. (Paul Chapman is also a person, now a member of the SAGE London Board, who came on as a non-executive director after the acquisition.)

From 1998, we grew Paul Chapman rapidly and successfully, particularly the education list, to nearly 10 times the size now than it was when we acquired it 10 years ago. The acquisition was also important in bringing in people with expertise in this field. When we took over the company, we hired everyone who was in it. The key person, Marianne Lagrange, who was the editorial director of Paul Chapman Publishing, is still a part of the SAGE London team. Paul Chapman was a very successful acquisition and opened up the doors to a new discipline for publishing out of SAGE London. (See Chapter 11, pp. 147–150, for Stephen Barr's report of SAGE London in the new millennium.)

CHAPTER 10

Changing Course

New Leadership, Culture, and Direction

In 1984, we began thinking seriously about succession plans. It was clear that the company was growing beyond a point at which I felt comfortable continuing to be its president. For one thing, we were getting a bit too bureaucratic, and I was getting further and further away from doing what I enjoyed—namely, being a publisher, making the decision to publish, and putting our company's marketing commitment behind the products that I had developed.

We were fortunate in that my oldest stepson, David McCune, had been on SAGE, Inc.'s Board of Directors since the mid-1980s. He had watched us grow over time and became more and more interested in the publishing business and its challenges while somewhat less enchanted with his own business.

David joined SAGE at the beginning of 1988, and by September 1989, he followed George as President of SAGE. I had served as President and CEO for nearly two decades and then became Chairman and Publisher while George served as President and Publisher for more than five years. In just under two years, David had gotten a very thorough baptism in the business of running a publishing house, the short time period made possible by the experience he'd gained in serving on our Board since 1985—and also because he is a very smart cookie. The track record in terms of growth was very dramatic over the decade of David's presidency. He also helped lay the foundation for future growth and change.

Handing Over the Reins

George and I very clearly intended at the outset to create the foundation of a business that would achieve $20 to $25 million in sales and be profitable at the before-tax profit rate of a minimum of 10% per annum. We thought 12% or 15% was certainly achievable. Some college textbook publishers (in those days) could generate profits closer to 20% annually before tax, but we were not in the textbook business at that time. We were doing academic journals and books in the social and behavioral sciences. (SAGE, Ltd was doing much the same but at that time still had a very small list of journals, and profits there had not yet achieved double digits but were clearly headed toward hitting that mark shortly.) We had built the foundation to achieve those goals and more.

The story of how we built our list of products and expanded SAGE during the 1960s, 1970s, and 1980s has been told in Chapters 3 through 7. To summarize, we had started many journals from scratch, some were scholarly association journals for which we had long-term publishing contracts, and others were journals that we acquired from academics who had gotten tired of self-publishing or were getting older, thinking of retirement, and looking for an exit strategy themselves. We were also publishing social science books and edited volumes, as well as reference books, like the *Handbook of Sociology* and a cluster of handbooks in the field of communication (all were great successes in terms of reviews and sales). In addition, we did monographs and books that could be used as texts at a graduate level. The texts sold to libraries and niche graduate class markets—we'd sell 7 copies for one class and maybe 12 copies for another. Perhaps we'd pick up 50 to 100 such course "adoptions" for a year (or two). But at the time, we'd been used to selling most of our book titles as single copies to libraries, so those few graduate classroom sales actually made a rather pleasant and profitable change.

George and I certainly felt that those foundations were strong and solid. We also knew that the company, in order to grow beyond its 1988 level, would have to *change*. The decision as to what the new goals should be, and therefore what the changes in strategy should be, clearly needed to be set by the next generation of leaders and, in particular, by David McCune, to whom we were handing over the reins and the responsibility.

Growth in the 1990s

David's immediate objective was to grow the company to the point where it was selling $100 million or more a year in product, taking the company to twice its size at the time he became President. He did give some thought to the possibility of going public but decided after a few years—and some strenuous objections from me—that independence was better, and we should focus on organic growth (as well as acquisitions) and other ways of getting working capital, including increasing our credit facility with our bank.

Looking at the profits after 1990, it's important to note that in the publishing business, the next year or two is pretty much set in concrete. The process can take a while. We have to sign contracts for publishing with authors and editors a few years prior to publication and then struggle to get the manuscripts out of the college professors or public policy makers (also busy Ph.D.s with multiple obligations), who might or might not feel that meeting their deadlines is a critical task. An analogy would be turning a tanker around in the middle of the ocean. It can't be done in one short mile, just as changing the course of a publishing company (without a major acquisition) can't be done in only one year—generally it takes two or three. (In hindsight, perhaps David wished he had invested in adding to our editorial acquisition capability a little sooner than he did; however, under his stewardship, we clearly went in the right direction.)

Something else we did in the 1990s under David's leadership (in addition to continuing to support and encourage the growth and expansion of SAGE London) was to find new imprints that covered areas not already covered by SAGE Publications. One of these is a separate imprint, Corwin Press, which publishes products for school administrators; another is Pine Forge Press, which focuses on college textbooks. The lead time to profitability in those fields is a lot longer than in journal publishing and quite a lot longer with college texts, as we knew.

One of the lessons we learned early on is to always remember that "cash is king." For the first 15 to 20 years of SAGE, Inc.'s existence, and certainly in the first five years of our subsidiaries' existences, we focused on cash flow with even more of an eagle eye than we did the P&Ls. I learned that lesson early and learned it well, and it is so internalized now that I don't think I can ever forget it.

In addition, we felt (after looking at some of our competitors in publishing and even at some of our subsidiaries) that in some businesses, too much capital can ruin you. I tend to urge people to be very cautious about how much capital they get in the early days and how they spend it. Our neighbor Amgen in Thousand Oaks, California, is probably one of the best examples I know of a company that raised a lot of money through IPOs (initial public offerings) but then very intelligently, to my way of thinking, squirreled most of it away and was fairly parsimonious at doling it out. They also had some real hits with a couple of their earliest products!

Perhaps it's best in the early phase of a business to behave as if you don't have much capital behind you. We had no trouble doing that since, in fact, that was reality. Having started the company in 1965 with $500, half of which was the valuation of a used air conditioner, rather than money in a bank account, I had no trouble at all feeling cash poor!

A Sudden Turn and Move

Nine months after David became President of SAGE, in May of 1990, George died of cardiac disease. It was a sudden death, and the family was shattered.

It was a very difficult time for all of us. George and I had been married almost 24 years, and we had just begun to talk about our 25th wedding anniversary. We wanted it to be held in Yosemite, at our cabin where we spent so many happy and productive times, but it was not to be. Instead, he died there while I was in Canada on a brief business trip.

We had three memorial services for George. One was held soon after his death in Malibu Canyon at a ranch where we sometimes had company events. Another was organized by Jerry Kaplan in New York in the autumn of that year. I had a small private memorial service that summer at our cabin in Yosemite, mostly for family and close friends from Wawona and nearby Oakhurst. After the service, David, my younger daughter Susan, and I scattered the ashes. It was hard on all of us, a difficult period in the family. David's wife, Susan Watt, was facing serious surgery at the time, and Doug, their son, was only 8½ years old. All four of George's children were shocked as well as grief stricken.

It was over a year until I made any decision about where I would live. For 20 years, from 1966 to 1986, George and I had kept the ever-growing SAGE offices in Beverly Hills, while living in an adjacent neighborhood. In 1986, we had moved SAGE's offices and ourselves up the coast to Thousand Oaks in Ventura County, where we lived together until George died. Then, in the spring of 1992, I started looking around.

I knew I didn't want to go back to Los Angeles, so I looked for a house in the Santa Barbara area and found what I wanted in nearby Montecito. I had always lived in fairly large cities, except for my year in Oxford, so this would be a change, but the beauty of Santa Barbara and the depth of my friendships here were compelling (see Chapter 13 for mention of my extended Santa Barbara family). In addition, the Los Angeles International Airport is only 90 miles away, a factor important to me as I do quite a bit of international travel. I had Thanksgiving in my new home in 1992 with Jerry Kaplan as my house guest and celebrated the holidays that year with many of my friends at UCSB along with those of our family living in California.

About a year after George's death, knowing I'd be moving soon, I was cleaning out a closet and came across a yellow sheet of paper. On it, George had written a prediction of what the company's next five years of sales revenues would be, and that first year, he turned out to be right on target. I gave the piece of paper to Matt Jackson in London and kept photocopies, and together we ticked off the subsequent years. George was right on target with his forecast, matching our actual figure during a period of time when SAGE was doubling profits and sales every five years.

To his credit, David McCune was President during that time, and he was clear about meeting sales and profit targets but also about how he wanted the company culture to be. I think he was very successful in fulfilling both of those ambitions, but I will let David tell the story of how he led SAGE in the time he was President, expanding our products and acquisitions, creating a management team, and implementing a culture change to take SAGE through the last decade of the 20th century into the new millennium.

Reflections: David F. McCune

New Directions

In the late 1980s, during a family visit at George and Sara's cabin in Yosemite, I remember sitting around the dining room table at dinner and asking my father how SAGE was doing. I had been on the Board since 1985, but in this informal setting, I wanted to hear what his more personal thoughts were. He told me he was considering retiring (he'd had open heart surgery in 1982) and that he and Sara were looking at a succession plan, possibly selling the company (although that was not what either of them really wanted to do). In response, with not much forethought, I said that I might be able to make a contribution. The idea occurred to me like a challenge at the time, something I wasn't getting from the work I was doing, which was consulting as a software programmer.

George looked across the table at me, apparently shocked by my offer, and said simply, "Really?" As I thought about it further, and George and Sara considered the possibility of me taking over the leadership of the company, I became more interested. Then, in 1988, I came on board, and by late 1989, I became the President of SAGE.

Right away, there were a number of challenges to be met, most of them due to the growth that the company had experienced and the need for a new structure of management to support that growth. While there were as many as 90 employees in California at the time, there were very few who had any kind of managerial independence. Most in management had no idea what their budget was, information that had been available only to Sara and George, and so they didn't know how to manage a budget. Neither was anyone good at hiring or developing new staff, another function that had been largely centralized.

I knew right away that I needed to build a management team that would help me run the ship. When George and Sara were at the helm, because there were two of them, they had 48 hours in a day to get the job done. I had only me to do both their jobs, and I wasn't about to try to make decisions about every aspect of the business. There simply wasn't enough time. Plus, I knew I could never grow the company beyond a certain size if it remained centralized in vital management functions. I needed a team.

I also recognized that building a team would involve a major shift in the company's culture in the way people related to each other. One way of managing people that did not work back then was jumping the chain of command. This happened when people in high positions gave feedback to junior people without first going to the junior person's department head, a demoralizing experience for both the person in charge and the junior person under him or her. I knew I had to change that style of management if I was going to have a strong team of people with whom I could work.

What I saw as my first task, more than directing which authors we should sign or what the direct mail brochures should look like (even though those are core issues), was to build a management team that would have the skills to make important decisions on their own. This would involve altering the culture of the company, as well as providing new access to information and training.

My management training prior to coming on board was zero. I could only bring to the task common sense and my prior work experience, some of which was quite valuable as it turned out. I had spent a few years at Time, Inc. as a journalist, and I'd been impressed with the company culture. Management made it clear that they were privileged to have us and, at the same time, we were privileged to be there. I remember thinking when I left Time that I would never, for the rest of my life, work at a place as good as that. Now, in a position to make changes, I wanted to shape SAGE in the same direction, to build a company where people, including myself, could truly say it's a privilege to be working here.

In building my management team, I started out to find bright people. But even more, I knew the key lay in organizing people in such a way that the sum of what they could produce was greater than the sum of each individual's efforts. I'd learned this lesson from working for a short time at AT&T in Rutherford, New Jersey, as a contract programmer in the Bell Labs division. Bell Labs had produced some of the greatest genius products in communication history.

I remember coming home in the evening and saying to my wife, "Another day went by and I still haven't met the people who invented the phone system. They must keep them behind a locked door, because the guys I've been working with don't have the kind of genius to produce such brilliant inventions." I learned from my experience at Bell Labs that simply having bright people on board wasn't enough. The real magic happens when you create an environment where those people can interact and bounce off each other to produce something that's over and above the sum of their individual efforts. I wanted to create such an environment at SAGE.

I set about accomplishing my vision by first interviewing each one of the 90 employees in the California-based headquarters. I also spent extensive time with senior managers in London and New Delhi. I wanted to know who was who and what it was that motivated each one of them to come to work at SAGE. Ultimately, I wanted to develop a mission for people to embrace, such that they would be inspired and strive to do their best, because they knew their efforts were making the world a better place.

Given the nature of the business, an inspiring mission wasn't so hard to figure out. Back then, SAGE was primarily a social sciences publisher, disseminating educational information. I'm a firm believer in the goodness of free-market democracy, and the education system is the foundation of that—without education, democracy doesn't work. I wanted the people at SAGE to understand that education is the business we're in, not selling widgets and not, even worse, selling a product that kills people, like cigarettes. Ours is a product that educates people and makes a better life possible for many, and this was an important part of our mission.

I believed that being an employee at SAGE was an opportunity for everyone to know that they made a difference. We sell thousands of copies of a book that some people may read or use to study and pass a test.

Some of them will actually think about the content and possibly change what they do for a living, how they do their job, or whether they get a Ph.D. or not—even what their political views are. Compared with working for Phillip Morris, selling cigarettes, having a job where you can make that kind of a difference is not a bad deal!

I wanted to infuse people with a sense that what we do, publishing books by and for educators, is sacred. Connecting with people on a personal level was a first step. As I went around and interviewed people at SAGE, I mentally divided up those who cared and those who didn't. This was how I started out to build a culture grounded in a passionate mission that all could share.

Another challenge I faced when I came on board was perhaps more mundane, but related to culture and how people experienced working at SAGE. This concerned the sheer mechanics of getting people to run their particular part of SAGE in a professional way, efficiently as well as thoughtfully. A problem was, as I mentioned, no one knew the budget for their own department, but even more, no one other than a few people in accounting knew what the annual sales of the company were. That information had been a closely held company secret. I felt everyone in the company should know, so I started holding monthly company-wide meetings and using an overhead projector (no PowerPoint in those days) put up the financial reports to show the entire company what the sales and profits looked like.

I had to argue with George a bit at first. He was worried our competitors would find out how big we were and that employees wouldn't understand where our profits went. But I believed it didn't matter if competitors found out—they probably knew anyway. As for the employees—even those who didn't make a lot of money—when I showed them the profits for the year, I went to some effort to explain what was done with that money. They needed to understand that we were not owned by a huge conglomerate, so if we didn't have a profit, we'd be out of business. I also explained that we didn't live extravagantly at SAGE, and in the early 1980s and 1990s, we certainly didn't. No one was driving around in a Rolls Royce—George and Sara may have had a Jaguar they'd owned for a decade. We had no corporate jet, no 120-foot sailboat. I explained how we put all the profit back into the company, and if there wasn't any profit, we'd have to declare bankruptcy and all go home.

A legitimate question that arose was, *Why should we grow?* We were maybe $15 million in revenue back then, and people would question me about why we should get any bigger. My answer was simple and to the heart of our mission: *What we do is sacred and therefore our business is worth growing.* We publish educational material, we help people learn, and that is good for democracy. Why shouldn't we try, with all of our effort, to pursue that purpose twice or 10 times as much? If we don't grow and make a profit, we go out of business, and there will be graduate students whose lives will be impacted. There will be fields of study, several of which SAGE was instrumental in launching, which would no longer exist or exist in a diminished way. The world won't be as good a place to live in—so we have to grow, and to grow means the business also must be profitable.

An Environment of Respect

In building our corporate culture, I wanted to create an environment where there was a deep respect for the people who worked there. We spend more of our waking hours with our colleagues at work than we do at home with our children, so it's an important relationship. When I left Time, Inc., after working there only a couple of years, I felt I was a better writer, and a better and more confident human being than when I had walked in the door. I got an extraordinarily good education on a deeply personal level, and I'll always be grateful to my editor-in-chief there.

Similarly, I wanted each person at SAGE to feel deeply respected and become more self-confident than when they walked in the door. Self-confidence is one of the other cornerstones of democracy, as is self-respect, which comes from feeling you can make a difference and that your opinion counts. People can so easily feel beaten down in their work experience, and I hoped that when they left SAGE (if they did), they would have increased self-respect and confidence from their experience of working with us.

To create such an environment, I did a number of things. We started an education reimbursement program to pay for an employee's tuition—100% if they took a course of study that had anything remotely to do with our business and 50% if they took nonrelated courses. We've been very proud of people at SAGE who went off to night school, some to get their GED, others to get a B.A. We only had to pay for it, a small part, compared with studying and doing the homework, which is a huge challenge for someone with a full-time job, a family, and other responsibilities.

Another way I saw to build confidence and self-respect was to offer opportunities to people within the company who were not only capable but willing to be trained. Back then, as growth was taking off, we had the need and the challenge to educate new middle managers, so we started the SAGE Publishing College to train people and move them up. After recommendations were made by department managers, we'd select 10 to 12 people who would take a week out of their job to learn about the business and be taught by myself and senior management. Occasionally we roped in a nearby bookseller or librarian to join our "faculty" for a day. The college also provided a way for senior management to observe those 12 people in action, and then make joint decisions about future promotions. Many of our "graduates" are now key members of our middle management team in either California or London.

To bring about more unification in the company, something I felt would contribute to the growing culture, I began to hold company-wide informational meetings. People knew what their own department was doing, but not what other departments did—other than to be the source of some of their headaches! To overcome this gap, every month, I had one department explain to the rest of the company what they did. Production people would present about how a book manuscript came in and got turned into a book. Accounts payable had no idea how that happened, and neither did customer service, so every department rotated around over a period of a year.

At that time, we had grown to about 250 people. We could have done our company-wide meetings on video, but it was important to me that the whole company come together and meet each other, meet me. Even though it's all about business—I might be telling them why we have to cut the budget—there was still a personal, heartfelt message I often wanted to deliver.

Something I felt strongly about early on at SAGE was for me, as CEO, to spend time talking to people and getting to know them, even after my initial phase of interviewing the entire staff. I'm not a gregarious person—I'm happy to spend four weeks sailing by myself in the middle of the ocean, not talking to anyone—so this wasn't easy for me. But I knew it was essential, both to find out what's going on in the building and to get a feel for things. I believe that if there's one single thing a CEO can never delegate, it's the creation and maintenance of the corporate culture. That is the CEO's job and nothing else. If you do delegate that job, then your absence becomes a part of the culture—that the CEO doesn't care.

I took it upon myself every day to be out into the cubicles where people were working to try and get my message across—about our mission statement, about how important what we do is, and about why doing it well is so important. In any company, there are unpleasant parts, as in life, so it's important to repeat and get people to understand how valuable what they're doing is, because we can easily forget.

I also wanted to create a place where people felt reasonably safe so they could contribute creatively without fear of being criticized. I tried to foster creativity as part of building management. This meant ensuring that the chain of command—how people received criticism or feedback—followed in departmental channels that built commitment, self-respect, and a desire to always do better. I had to be where people were actually working to do this, to monitor and encourage so that relationships would be of this nature, and to handle any missteps that resulted in damage to relationships.

Creating Corporate Unification

A big challenge I faced during my presidency was improving the relationship between SAGE, Inc. in California and SAGE, Ltd in London, two offices that saw each other as sources of each other's problems. There were many communications by fax between people (before e-mail), but basically, they didn't like each other very much. There were disagreements on how to do things, like the marketing of a book or journal. To resolve this, I instituted a change and required that all senior managers, on both sides, spend a week once a quarter at the other office.

Initially, this met with some resistance, as it meant crossing the Atlantic four times a year. *What do you want us to talk about?* they'd ask me. I'd tell them that if they were done with business after two days, they should take in a Dodgers game or go out to a restaurant together, anything to get to know each other. Once I took the senior people from London and California down to San Diego on a management retreat, and after we were done with business, we rented a Jet Ski fleet on the bay and just had fun with each other. I'd often choose recreational activities that no one person could outshine the others at. I wanted them to depend on each other and interact, which required everyone to be equally ungraceful. These kinds of activities eventually started to shift relationships between the two places, helping people to be more friendly and cooperative.

Expanding With New Affiliates

In mid-1990, we launched Corwin Press with a vision to assist administrators and teachers to be more effective in schools. Today Corwin offers practical, hands-on resources to help PreK–12 education professionals do their work better and, in the process, helps advance the field and improve education for all learners. Corwin publishes an array of practitioner-friendly books on such important topics as educational leadership, in regular and special education, curriculum development, multicultural education, and education law.

Back then, I was starting from scratch and there were zero titles on our list. I hired Gracia Alkema to build the imprint. (Sara reminds me that we stole Gracia from Jossey-Bass, hoping also to get her husband C. Terry Hendrix back, because he'd been our editorial director. It worked and we got them both, Terry as a Vice President for SAGE, and Gracia as President of our new imprint for education professionals, Corwin Press.)

Gracia helped build Corwin Press by finding out what was needed and what the customers wanted. She (and sometimes myself) talked to the school teachers first, or the principals, or the superintendents. Our customers at Corwin are administrative educators, staff development people and teachers, and if a day went by that there wasn't one of those people visiting or being visited, talking to Gracia or other staff, I considered the day a failure. I believed it was very important for staff to stay in touch with the customer and inspired about what they were doing. Teachers are pretty inspiring people, even though some may be burned out. But in general, it's energizing to be with educators who are on the front lines. I sent Corwin staff to go into schools frequently, even though we'd also go to the major conferences and do other market research. Similarly at SAGE, there are acquisition editors who go out into the field, because it's important to the company that we stay connected to the people we are serving.

Today, Allyson P. Sharp is the Editorial Director of Corwin Press, and the revenue from Corwin is from a completely different bucket—PreK–12 schools—than revenue from SAGE, which is primarily from higher education markets; this is a way to spread our resources around and obtain multiple income streams. In its very beginning, Corwin was in the same building as SAGE Publications, but today it is housed separately in another building, although in the same complex. I've always wanted to keep the two entities separate, which in general, I think is a good thing, even though it does mean that the President (Corwin reports to Blaise Simqu) needs to make an extra effort to know what goes on there.

Not long after Gracia got started with Corwin in 1991, we started Pine Forge Press. I was approached by an editor, Steve Rutter from Wadsworth, one of the top companies publishing freshman- and sophomore-level books in social sciences. He pointed to something I'd been thinking, which was that there was an undergraduate market, the junior/senior college levels, that the big textbook companies ignored, because the class size is too small for them. They all had big sales forces and couldn't support them if the average sale was only 30 to 40 books. Steve suggested that SAGE ought to be doing books at a lower level, because the higher graduate levels were getting smaller. His idea was for SAGE to combine our direct mail with telephone sales calls without having a sales force, so we could develop books for the mid-level undergraduate curriculum and sell them successfully. I was interested from day one, and I believed exactly what he was telling me.

We did a business plan and he came on board to start what became Pine Forge Press. There were no books when he came on—again, we started from scratch—and sitting in my office where I could watch and learn how he did it, Steve signed the first book. It was a different model of publishing, using telemarketing, talking directly to the professors rather than direct mailing them. Steve was very good at it, because he'd been the editorial director at Wadsworth and knew how to develop books with authors.

This new development was just what SAGE needed, because with the collapse of the research monograph, we needed to move down to reach the undergraduate market. As Pine Forge Press grew, Steve, who was an excellent editor, figured out what the curriculum was at the colleges, what books and topics were on the rise, and where there'd be more enrollments in certain courses. He was also good at dealing with authors and working to get a book that other professors would need and want. We ran into problems later when we started to get bigger and more management challenges arose; then, after I left, Steve chose to leave as well.

By then, SAGE Publications had seriously begun to shift its own editorial policy, becoming more like Pine Forge, because Pine Forge showed that the model worked. SAGE had been doing mostly research books, and I could see we'd have to move our books lower down on the curriculum. Pine Forge made that move, and made it well. Soon, the argument for having Pine Forge as a separate company went away. Today, SAGE also does what Pine Forge used to do and Pine Forge is now a SAGE imprint; there is no separate corporation called Pine Forge.

Another imprint I got started in my tenure was Outside the Box. A couple came to me with supplemental reading books for K–3 that they had self-published, and I liked the product. I also liked the market because it wasn't basal readers, which had to get adopted by school districts. These were supplements that teachers would buy, and it was back in the whole-language days. The problem was that whole language as a way of teaching reading was beginning to decline by the mid-1990s, and this couple and their books were committed to whole language as a reading method. Their follow-up series of books didn't ever do very well. I don't know if I'd stayed at SAGE that I could have convinced them to do other kinds of supplemental books, not so committed to one particular ideology, but the choice was made after I left SAGE, with the original founding editors buying it and moving to another region.

There were two other start-ups during the time I was President of SAGE. One was a newsletter publishing operation headed by Tim Baskerville. It was managed from the United States and operated in London, but did not become a core business. The other start-up was in software distribution and was named Scolari. This was interesting and complemented our research methods publishing. But neither growth nor profits met expectations, so we moved on.

The Vision Continues

During the period of David's transformative leadership, I was fortunate to meet Jon Goodman, and I think she shared considerable sagacity with us during her interview, which I quote here:

Jon Goodman, SAGE Inc. Board of Directors and President, Town Hall, Los Angeles

I've known Sara and been on the Board of SAGE, Inc. for 15 years. I first met Sara when I was Chair of the Entrepreneur Program at USC, and I am currently President of Town Hall, Los Angeles, which is a large public forum. I've been involved in venture capital, funding high technology, rapidly growing companies, as a general partner and advisor, and I've also served on many Boards over the years.

SAGE is now a little more than 10 times larger than it was in 1994. I watched it and participated in it—banged my fists on the table a couple of times. This kind of growth is not usual. I have been involved with many rapidly growing companies, and most that go through a growth phase as steady and consistent as SAGE have sooner or later blown up somewhere. SAGE has not. SAGE has gotten consistently more sophisticated and consistently more organized over the years.

In the 1990s, David McCune as President understood what was happening in the world and behaved appropriately when he reacted to the many changes. In 1992, the World Wide Web was invented, and one of the advantages of SAGE is that there were two Board Members, Peter Lyman and myself, who were intimately involved with the Internet. I helped write the business plans that took ARPANET to the Internet in 1989 (I was part of a very large national team; I didn't do it alone). Peter, who is now deceased, built the electronic library at USC, was chief librarian at UC Berkeley, and was an Associate Dean in the UC Berkeley School for Information Science. In 1995, I opened the Annenberg Project at USC, which was an Internet research facility.

We were the genuine experts, and we knew what was coming. But that doesn't mean David McCune wasn't an excellent student who grasped very quickly what the implications were going to be, and he rode it well.

I've known Sara in a lot of contexts, and aside from the fact that she's a good publisher, she is a clear-eyed and dispassionate observer. I have been around people who build extraordinary businesses all my working life, and this is a characteristic of successful businesspeople.

Reflecting on David's story, I'm prompted to say that in the 1990s, internationally and at home, SAGE Publications expanded and transformed on a scale George and I could not have envisioned back in the mid-1980s. We knew then there was a need for change, but we did not foresee how, in a little more than 10 years, the company would go from being mainly a social science pub-lisher to a publisher that also included a wide range of periodicals in subfields of science, technology, engineering, and medicine—and more. Under the Corwin Press imprint, we began to offer an ever-expanding list of books for teachers and professionals in preschool thorough high school teaching and education; Pine Forge heralded our entry into the college textbook publishing business, causing us to reinvent ourselves as a viable business in tune with current and upcoming markets and trends. The initiatives that resulted in such an explosion of growth and transformation were based on the foresight and leadership of David McCune, President of SAGE from 1988 until 1998.

Beginning in 1995, as my day-to-day workload at SAGE Publications decreased, and I fully relocated to Santa Barbara, I began to nurture another long-held dream. I took on several philanthropic responsibilities, primarily through our family foundation, the McCune Foundation, and the Foundation Board of the University of California at Santa Barbara.

The McCune Foundation was established by George and me in 1990, just months before George passed away. The original plan was for the Foundation to support projects in the United States, the UK, and India, where SAGE had offices, such as providing books for university students in India and London and helping set up medical clinics or dig wells in rural India. However, the focus of the Foundation shifted over the first decade, partially under the influ-ence of early Board member Marilyn Gittell and also later with additional insights from Board member Sandra Ball-Rokeach, both strong advocates for a new kind of collaborative effort involved with building social capital. This approach emphasizes that grassroots efforts of organizations, not individuals, can build power to be used in the public sphere.

By the end of the 1990s, the Foundation was no longer directing efforts toward individual charity and service delivery but moving in the direction of building community capacity locally in low-income communities of Ventura and Santa Barbara Counties, to encourage people to organize themselves in pursuing policies to suit their needs. The coming new millennium would usher in a decade of business growth and philanthropic giving that would exceed all expectations. (See Chapter 12 for more on the McCune Foundation and other philanthropic activities.)

PART IV

The Millennium and Beyond

CHAPTER 11

New Millennium Update

In the first 10 years of the new millennium, with offices in the United States (Thousand Oaks, California, and Washington, D.C.), the United Kingdom (London), India (New Delhi), and the Asia-Pacific region (Singapore and Beijing), the size of SAGE Publications has doubled. Today, at the end of the first decade of the new millennium, there are more than 1,000 employees in offices spread across four continents. Our mission to inform and educate a global community of scholars, practitioners, researchers, and students now spans a wide range of subject areas, including social sciences, business and management studies, humanities, and science, technology (engineering), and medicine. During the past 10 years especially, SAGE has been on a path to becoming the leading privately owned international publisher of journals, books, and electronic media for academic, educational, and professional markets.

This phenomenal growth and achievement could only have been possible with the outstanding leadership of very special people and their total commitment to our mission. These people include the current President and CEO of SAGE Publications, Inc., Blaise Simqu; Stephen Barr, Managing Director of London and President of SAGE International; and Vivek Mehra, Managing Director of SAGE India. I include the words of Blaise Simqu and Stephen Barr in this chapter to update us on the many achievements and milestones we have reached with their leadership and the dedication of those working close to them in the new millennium, contributing to the growth of the company internationally.

Changing Leadership and Continuing Traditions

In September 1998, David McCune left the company, and I was interim President for a year until we hired Michael Melody as President of SAGE for the next five years. With his great background in college text publishing from his prior career at Houghton-Mifflin, Mike grew the business. Upon Mike's retirement in mid-2005, Blaise Simqu took over the leadership of SAGE, Inc.

I originally hired Blaise in 1986. He was a graduate of UCLA and had some publishing experience but not in scholarly publishing. He started out at SAGE, Inc. as a Production Manager and then, on his own efforts, became our Political Science Editor, working with the Goods and Greats like Marilyn Gittell and Benjamin Barber (two founders of important journals on our list). At that point, he was handling both the journals and the book portfolio in political science. He left in 1990 to go to San Francisco and court Erin, who subsequently became his wife. While he was in the Bay Area, Blaise worked at Jossey-Bass. He came back to us in 1996 via Kinko's (owned by a Montecito local, Paul Orfalea), where he met Tracy Ozmina, who became our Chief Information Officer (now senior Vice President). Blaise became Vice President of the Journals Division and then Executive Vice President, and then was promoted in 2005 to President and CEO of SAGE. Blaise is one of the few people still in the building at SAGE who actually knew George.

Looking back over a period of 45 years, I am proud to say we've only had six CEOs: myself, George McCune, David Brooks, David McCune, Michael Melody, and now Blaise Simqu. I believe that the low number reflects the culture of a company where people come to work and stay because they can make a creative difference and are recognized for their contribution.

Certainly Blaise has fostered the tradition of company culture that David McCune started at SAGE in the 1990s. One example of that tradition, ongoing for more than two decades, is the honoring of employees who have stayed with SAGE for a number of years. Since he was appointed President and CEO, Blaise has graciously and generously hosted a dinner each year at his home that has come to be known as the "Tenure Dinner." This catered and elegant dinner, usually held during the month of September, is intended to extend thanks and appreciation for all SAGE employees who have achieved 10 years or more with SAGE in the United States.

In 2009, there were a total of 82 employees who were celebrating 10 or more years with the company. Of special note at this past September 2009 tenure dinner, there were 10 employees who celebrated 20 or more years with SAGE:

- Claudia Hoffman, Managing Editor, Books Production (20 years)
- Ron Siquig, Material Handler II (20 years)
- Barbara Hake, Receptionist (21 years)
- Joyce Walker, Associate Production Editor (21 years)
- Linda Milbrett, Office Services Clerk (22 years)
- Ron Marcelino, Warehouse Assistant Supervisor (23 years)
- Astrid Virding, Senior Project Editor (23 years)
- Herman Lambey, Facility Services Clerk (24 years)
- LeRoy Diggs, Locations Coordinator (26 years)
- Sylvan Mejia, Credit Specialist II (27 years)

In addition to honoring 10-year veterans, an incredibly rich and unique benefit is in place at SAGE, which is the awarding of anniversary trips for all employees who reach five-year milestone anniversaries with SAGE (specifically, every five years, i.e., upon the 5-, 10-, 15-, 20-, and 25-year anniversaries). The employee is provided with the opportunity to travel to one of the other SAGE geographical locations. For Thousand Oaks, California–based employees, that includes Washington, D.C., London, England, New Delhi, India, and Singapore. SAGE pays the cost of two airline tickets for the employee plus one travel companion, along with awarding the employee an extra week's vacation and spending allowance, as well as a travel guide for the location they will be visiting and a leather passport holder. The only requirement is that they spend at least a half a day in the SAGE office in the location they are visiting, but other than that, they are free to explore and educate themselves as they wish. For some employees, they would never have had a passport or traveled to Europe had it not been for SAGE, and many long-lasting friendships have also been a result of these anniversary trips.

To give an update on the growth of the company, both fiscally and physically, I present Blaise's own words:

Reflections: Blaise Simqu

Financial Growth and More

The years between 1995 and 2005 were a period of fantastic growth and profit for SAGE. The company basically doubled in size twice during that time frame. Since 1996, we hit $100 million in sales; five years after that, we doubled and hit $200 million in sales. It took us almost 40 years to get to $100 million, and then it took us just five years to get to $200 million.

Many efforts and events have contributed to SAGE's growth. Primarily, it was the continued investment in the journals program and the expansion of our international programs that drove the phenomenal growth. David McCune can be credited with reemphasizing and clarifying the long standing financial and economic value of journals to the company. He and his management team, and subsequent management teams, began to acquire journals back in the 1990s that led the fast pace of growth.

When I came back to SAGE in 1996, the total sales that year were $40 million; today (end of 2009) sales of just the journals originated in the United States are well over $50 million, and that is roughly only half our revenues. The same growth factors were at work for the London-based operations. SAGE India and SAGE Asia-Pacific are also growing rapidly, as we had forecast. The mixture of internal growth, acquisitions, and expansion of our international sales efforts has fuelled and accelerated our operations globally, with great results in both sales and profitability. While the growth percentages slow in times of economic distress, education (and especially higher education) is needed and sought out during such times. That is when companies like ours see the strength of our core businesses enhanced. We have seen this happen before and, economic cycles being what they are, may well see it happen in the future.

New Acquisitions and Publishing Programs

During that time period, we were also launching a lot of new products and expanding our book publishing programs. Pine Forge and Corwin, both new imprints started under David McCune, grew up in the 1990s and have continued to do well. Corwin, started as a company in 1990 with $0 in revenue, is now a $25 million enterprise with approximately 40 employees (all in California).

Pine Forge redefined for us what a successful book publishing program needed to be in the 1990s as well as boosting us into the first part of the new century. Pine Forge had a concept about a certain type of textbook that could reach a specific segment of the market. Ultimately, we saw the success of Pine Forge and realized essentially that's what we needed our book publishing program to be in the United States, so SAGE's book publishing program essentially became what Pine Forge had modeled. That growth combined with launching our reference program in 2001 led to even faster growth for our books program. (For more on both Corwin Press and Pine Forge Press, see Chapter 10.)

Another new imprint, SAGE Reference, was launched in January 2001 with the vision of publishing authoritative reference works in the social sciences for the academic library market. As SAGE had canceled all monograph publishing by that time, a new books revenue stream was needed to support and enhance the early growth of our textbook program.

The first SAGE Reference products were published in 2002, led by the *Encyclopedia of Crime and Punishment,* a four-volume work that won numerous awards and achieved sales in excess of $900,000. In the following years, the list of encyclopedias grew and so did the awards, since over 40% of the titles published became award winners. Titles such as *The SAGE Encyclopedia of Social Science Research Methods,* the *Encyclopedia of Anthropology,* and the *Encyclopedia of Leadership* became top-selling works and were sold to over 70% of the academic libraries in the United States (as well as achieving strong international sales).

By 2006, the front list grew to 15 titles, and SAGE Reference was recognized as one of the leading reference publishers by *Library Journal.* It was also the year when SAGE Reference became the very first publishing partner for the Gale Virtual Reference Library (GVRL), an e-book aggregator, a deal that has since generated more than $2.2 million in revenue.

In the short time since the 2001 launch of SAGE Reference, more than 100 titles have been published, edited by world-class social science scholars and consisting of tens of thousands of articles written by over 30,000 academics worldwide. The imprint has generated over $22 million in global revenue and continues to be recognized as a leading social science reference publisher.

Journal Growth: Social Sciences and STM

Jayne Marks, Vice President and Journals Editorial Director, heads up a team of journal acquisition editors, who continue in the tradition of collaboration established early on by the McCunes in the early days of SAGE. As a team, discipline-focused in-house acquisition editors in both social sciences and STM travel extensively to meet with editors and societies, prospect at conferences, and present to our editorial boards and society prospects. Their mission is to cultivate contacts for potential acquisitions and build relationships with editors and societies already published through SAGE so they want to keep working with us.

Two recent developments have significantly expanded our already strong journals list in the social sciences. In 2009, we signed an agreement to partner with the American Sociological Association (ASA) to publish eight of its journals beginning in 2010 and 2012. The ASA, founded in 1905, is dedicated to advancing sociology as a scientific discipline and profession serving the public good. The journals are the *American Sociological Review* (ASA's flagship journal and the number-one-ranked journal in sociology), *Contemporary Sociology: A Journal of Reviews, Journal of Health and Social Behavior, Social Psychology Quarterly, Sociology of Education,* and *Teaching Sociology* (which rejoins SAGE after being initially launched by us and then transferring to ASA)—all to be published in 2010. *Sociological Methodology* and *Sociological Theory* are to be published by SAGE beginning in 2012.

The acquisition of these eight journals represents a major step both for SAGE and for the ASA, as reflected in the words of ASA Executive Officer

Sally Hillsman: "SAGE has long provided significant publishing support to sociology, and the leadership of the American Sociological Association seeks to ensure the Association's scholarly communication system that strengthens our discipline and contributes to the well-being of society. I am confident that ASA's partnership with SAGE will move us forward in achieving these goals."

In the same year, we signed a 10-year agreement with another important association in the field of social and behavioral science, the Association for Psychological Science (APS), to publish its four journals. APS, founded in 1988 as the American Psychological Society, has grown into a significant organization whose impact on national policy is well recognized. The science of psychology and the academic and scientific exchange valued by scholars in the field have advanced enormously over the past 20 years, inspired and shaped in no small way by the APS. It is a strong voice for psychology, including researchers, teachers, applied scientists, clinical scientists, students, and more. Its journals are among the best in the field. The titles of the journals SAGE will begin publishing in 2010 are *Psychological Science* (one of the most prestigious and highly cited journals in the field), *Current Directions in Psychological Science, Psychological Science in the Public Interest,* and *Perspectives on Psychological Science.*

Prior to the mid-1990s, SAGE had published journals mainly in the social and behavioral sciences and had never published in STM (science, technology, and medicine) areas, such as chemistry, biology, engineering, or the health sciences. In 1998, we had a couple of fitful starts when we tried to launch a few medical journals that were not the quality we expected them to be, but things changed when we had an opportunity to publish engineering journals. We started publishing from scratch with journals such as the *Journal of Vibration and Control* and other areas in materials science, which is a major segment of the engineering discipline. Then, we bought a journal in robotics engineering from MIT Press, which is still one of our very successful journals, *The International Journal of Robotics Research.* Then, in 1999, we won the contract to become the publisher of our first medical journal, the *Journal of Clinical Pharmacology.*

The real kick start for SAGE in the STM area was the acquisition of the company Technomic in 2001, with its line of 20 to 25 engineering journals, the flagship of which was the *Journal of Composite Materials,* a leading journal in the field. Until we successfully absorbed that acquisition, however, we did not allow any of our other affiliates, SAGE London or SAGE India, to get into STM publishing, because we weren't sure we could be competitive. Major competitors in that area include some real 800-pound gorillas, like Elsevier (based in the Netherlands but global in reach). We wanted to establish some experience by keeping our bets in one place, and keep a close eye on how well we handled this type of publishing program.

Then, in 2006, we had yet another opportunity and acquired a British company that published medical journals, Hodder's Arnold Journals. With these two acquisitions and their lists, plus our own periodicals, we became publishers of significance in STM. Today, we publish journals in such areas as orthopedic surgery, dental surgery, aesthetic surgery, and hand surgery. The number of medical and health science titles in our journals portfolio is now more than 100. In 2010, we will add eight more titles to this list, so we went from zero titles to more than 100—all journals, no books—in less than 15 years.

Here is a summary of our current journal publishing program:

SAGE, Inc.—From 2000–2010, SAGE, Inc. added 156 journals to our list, bringing the total number of journals currently published (including those that we have signed and will begin publishing in 2010) to 265. This includes 185 social science journals and 80 health and medicine (STM) journals. Of these, SAGE is the owner of 151 journals and co-owner of two journals. There are four additional journals that we have signed but won't begin publishing until either 2011 or 2012, bringing the total of signed journals to 269.

SAGE London—Including 2010 publications, the London office publishes 197 social science journals and 66 STM journals, a total of 263 (56 are society owned and 16 jointly owned; 125 SAGE owned).

SAGE India—All 28 titles are in social science (none as yet in STM).

Worldwide, as of 2010, SAGE publishes 556 journals, including 410 social science journals and 146 STM journals.

Digital and Electronic Publishing

The handwriting was very much on the wall in the mid- to late 1990s, making it clear to everyone, both in California and in London, that the future of the journals business and the dissemination of scholarly information would be in an electronic environment. Once we all started to see and experience the power of search engines, we could see how much more valuable they could make academic research. And at the beginning of the millennium, we started transitioning and building a platform for all of our journals, which is called SAGE Journals On Line (SJOL). An institution, or consortia of institutions, can now buy the entire electronic library of SAGE journals. Individuals also have access through subscription.

Over the past two years, we made the effort to put all reference material into an electronic platform, creating SAGE Reference Online (SRO). With regard to academic research, including peer-reviewed publications of scholarly work and reference publishing, it makes sense for all of that to be in a more dynamic electronic environment because of the access and ability to search the depth of material. The launch took place in early 2007, and the platform instantly won major awards from the library media. By the end of 2008, SRO and GVRL sales (our share of the Gale Research VRL revenues) were 45% of the total revenue for SAGE Reference. In 2009, the largest front list was published at 20 titles, including the award-winning *Encyclopedia of Play* and *Encyclopedia of Education Law.* It was also the year that 80 SAGE handbooks were added to SRO.

Looking into the future, we are building an exciting new database at Congressional Quarterly Press, which was our big East Coast book acquisition in May 2008. CQ is a textbook and reference publisher in political science. The new database will have no print product—it will be entirely electronic.

Current and Future Growth

For many years, our goal in terms of top line growth was to always achieve double-digit growth. During this global recession that began in 2008, we're growing at high single digits, but we haven't gone through a period of decline or disastrous loss. We have managed to maintain steady healthy growth, even though it's single-digit growth, and SAGE is accustomed to double-digit growth. Double-digit growth, of course, gets harder when a company gets to be the size SAGE is now, and so as SAGE continues to grow, it's natural that those milestones are more difficult to achieve. Our current executive team expects to grow the company at a minimum of between 5% and 10% each year, but with an eye toward growing the company at double-digit rates whenever possible in future years.

In sum, SAGE is doing remarkably well, and in the year 2009, which was such a difficult one economically for so many businesses, SAGE had one of its most profitable years ever!

International Update

Years ago, before the late 1990s, SAGE offices in the United States, London, and India all operated as separate entities. The initial efforts to change that and bring the company into a more united international entity were started in the late 1990s when David McCune set a precedent for annual meetings on a regular basis. In the past five years, we've made even more progress in that effort.

Today, senior executives meet monthly and quarterly. The entire budgeting process is a global exercise that begins in January of each year for the subsequent year, with a heavy push from August through November. Our corporate strategic planning process is now a global effort that includes the creation and management of a global operating plan each year. In the past five years, we've had significant technology investments that only could have occurred on a global scale. We manage our journals now not as separate companies publishing a list of journals but with truly global management of the journals, treating them as publication assets that are sold around the world to institutions and need to be managed from the customers' perspective on a single, globalized basis.

It's very common at any given time for individuals from either London or the United States to be in the other office, because there's so much work being done between the two. We've also taken an initiative to have production staff members who report in to the U.S. office but actually work in New Delhi. There's been a massive effort over the past 5 to 10 years to create one global organization acting strategically in a unified manner, as opposed to a series of provincial offices that were all held together because they existed under a single corporate umbrella.

Our expansion into Asia, starting with our first effort in India in mid-1981, has expanded significantly. In India, we are currently publishing books and journals in a program specifically for Asia, meaning the Indian subcontinent and other locations in South Asia. (SAGE India also distributes our books and journals in the Indian market.) Some of SAGE India's titles (books on business and management) appear under the Response imprint, which has had strong success in the region.

Our Asia-Pacific affiliate is an effort to expand further into eastern Asia. In Singapore, we have a marketing and sales office that distributes all of our products. Beijing is part of the Asia-Pacific affiliate based in Singapore. We have sales representatives in Japan, with plans to put more sales reps in offices throughout Asia, including Taiwan, Korea, and Australia. Hearing Sara talk about our first marketing efforts in Japan (by direct mail in the early 1970s), I am in awe of our growth and expansion.

World Tour, 2009

Early in the history of SAGE, George would make four trips a year to London, and I would join him at least twice. From 1980 onwards, we went to India once a year; after he died in 1990, I began going to India every other year, and then less, because by then business in India was very well established, and linkages between SAGE India and SAGE London were being strengthened. In subsequent years (with the establishment in 1986 of SAGE Asia-Pacific Pte in Singapore), SAGE International operations began reporting through SAGE London with Stephen Barr, as Group President, adding to his responsibilities. By then, I was going to the UK quarterly as well (and had been for over a decade). It is only recently (2007) that I cut my UK trips back to two or three a year and began videoconferencing for the winter board meeting regularly.

Today, as the company expands, I find it important to venture out to witness for myself the phenomenal global progress we've experienced in just the past decade.

I started on my most recent trip around the world on January 10, 2009, first stopping in Tokyo, Japan, and then going on to Singapore, Dhaka (Bangladesh), and both Delhi and Pune in India, before touching down in London and returning to California after 42 days out of the country. The purpose of my visit was both business and philanthropy; I also intended to meet SAGE staff, longtime friends, and business associates in each of our international offices, and also consult on a possible philanthropic project in Bangladesh.

After meeting with key partners, including our friends and book sales distributors at Maruzen, and my old friend (now retired) Sumio Saito and some of our new SAGE staff in Japan, including Haruhiko Ohata, Consortia/Library

Manager of SAGE Asia-Pacific, I went on to the Singapore office. There I met with Steve Golden and his entire staff, including Shayama Nafik, our Book Sales Support Manager at that location. It was also great to meet the legendary Rosalia (who spends much of her time in Beijing) and once again see Nicola, who worked for us at SAGE London and is now based in Malaysia. They briefed me on their activity in the region, and I shared my views on the economic and business outlook for 2009, reiterating the importance of the Asia-Pacific region as a key growth area for SAGE.

Next, I went to Bangladesh, accompanied by my Executive Assistant from California, Kate Wilde. It was a different experience from my first visit to Dhaka in the early 1990s, when I stayed with friends. But it was most interesting, as Dhaka has changed and grown in the interim. Then, we went on to India.

Accompanied by Kate Wilde and Judi Weisbart (a friend who joined us from Santa Barbara), I visited the new SAGE India office in New Delhi for the first time. We were welcomed by Vivek Mehra and his staff in the traditional way with the garland, the *tilak* (Hindu forehead mark), and lighting of the ceremonial oil lamp. I took a tour of the office and met (a few days later) with the various departments heads, and then met with all the employees at a staff lunch, where I expressed my joy and pride at being in India once again and applauded everyone for all their efforts. SAGE India has grown so much since 1981 and is now a key part of our group.

Stephen Barr was also present during my visit, having come over from London, and at a dinner hosted by him in my honor, the guest list included authors, editors, contributors, and friends of SAGE. I talked fondly about my association with Tejeshwar Singh over the years, and in TJ's memory, I announced another fellowship, this time in the field of social sciences. The three of us from California also went to Pune for a few days.

Our return trip (from India to California via London) was hastened by a snowstorm and Kate coming down with a mysterious ailment that turned out to be the flu. But not taking any chances, I accompanied her from India to London and put her on a plane to California ahead of me and then stayed over another night in London to have dinner with dear friends Marian and Matt Jackson.

In his own words, Stephen Barr reports about expansion in the London office from 1998 to 2009. (See Chapter 9 for growth in the 1990s and into the millennium, as well as further international expansion from Barr's point of view.)

Reflections: Stephen Barr

SAGE London Update

Like the American office, growth of the London enterprise in the period of the late 1990s through the first decade of the new millennium was fueled by the acquisitions of both new publishing companies and new journals. In 1998, Paul Chapman was acquired, and in 2006, another key acquisition was the Arnold Journals list.

Arnold was a small publishing program, part of a massive publisher in the UK called Hodder Headline that included some very good social science content and also good medical content. Hodder decided Arnold Journals was too small to be viable in its own right, so they put it up for sale. At that time, we had agreed that SAGE London could acquire medical content alongside California, and this list being published by Hodder was perfect for jump-starting medical publishing out of the UK With the blessing of the California Board, we bid for it very strongly in an aggressive auction and managed to get it and have done fabulously well with the list ever since. This acquisition, along with the earlier acquisition of Paul Chapman Press, were key movements, enlarging SAGE London's scope to include a strong program in education and jump-starting medical publishing out of the London office.

"The Year of Methods"—2009

An area SAGE focused on in 2009, around the world, was making better known our enduring presence and legacy in the field of research methods, culminating in what we've called "The Year of Methods."

Research methodology has been a fundamental publishing program at SAGE for a long period of time—referred to often as the "jewel in our crown." It has become the binding glue for the entirety of academia, crossing all boundaries in terms of geography, levels, and intellectual disciplines. Political scientists, sociologists, social psychologists—all need to use statistics or research design, and methodology has been one of the heartbeats of SAGE historically. SAGE shaped a lot of young impressionable scholars across the globe to utilize and feel comfortable with appropriate research methods and whole disciplines as a consequence. (See Chapter 5 for how SAGE shaped research methodology.)

In 2008, Ziyad Marar, Deputy Managing Director in the London office, took the initiative in pointing out to the entire SAGE group that while we are quite probably the best research methods publisher on the planet, we had not capitalized on our heritage. As a result, we decided to make 2009 "The Year of Methods," a year in which we would adopt a three-pronged approach to articulate and make visible our role in research methodology.

The first prong was to ramp up the amount of methods publishing we'd been doing, so we decided to sign up 100 new books in research methods, as well as bring out a series of new editions of some of SAGE's major textbooks in research methods, such as John Creswell's *Research Design* and Andy Field on *Discovering Statistics Using SPSS* (SPSS is the standard statistical package used in the social sciences), which is a fantastic seller out of the London office.

The second prong was to develop PR resources, the first of which was a small book of our own, compiled by John W. Creswell, that told the history of our contributions to research methods—*How SAGE Has Shaped Research Methods: A 40-Year History.* Another innovative resource was the creation of an online social networking community called MethodSpace to publicly strengthen SAGE's visibility in the field. SAGE would support the site, help to organize and market it, and encourage people to join, but it wouldn't be centered around SAGE, per se.

MethodSpace is now up and is a free site, available on the Web (www .methodspace.com) to anyone who wishes to join. People can create forums on it to discuss the methodological problems that they are interested in and also get other people interested in those problems by commenting and advising. By September 2009, we were targeting

500 members, and at the end of 2009, there were 3,500 members with representatives from 149 countries around the world who have joined and use the site. We've created a much needed space where people can converge and, in doing so, have cemented our place as the publisher that supports the research methods community to succeed.

The third and final prong of our approach in "The Year of Methods" was to focus on building a new product base in which our research methods would be made available in an electronic format. We are working on creating a product called SAGE Research Methods Online, a database of research method–related content, which would be a tool for academics and research students and, to some extent, undergraduates in the range of social science disciplines. It is now well advanced in conception, and we'll have a beta test version in the middle of 2010, with a more formal official launch at the end of 2010 and beginning of 2011.

Building a Management Team

At the time I became Managing Director in 1996, we had on board other directors who had been part of the business for some time, including Matt Jackson as a non-executive director, Lynn Adams as Finance and Administration Director, Ian Eastment as Marketing Director, and Mike Birch as IT Director. Gradually over time, we got to the point where the company's needs had outgrown those roles and required a broader group of specialist directors, so progressively over time, Lynn, Ian, and Mike left between 1998 and 2004. Matt also retired as an outside director during that period but served as a consultant to me for a time during the transition.

With the expansion of the company into the Asia-Pacific market in 2007, my title has changed to include President of SAGE International, a role that gives me oversight over the Indian and Asia-Pacific offices, in addition to London. As I'm away from the UK frequently, much of the day-to-day management of the London company is in the hands of Ziyad Marar and Katharine Jackson. Together, the three of us are the UK members of the Global Executive Committee, a group of directors coming from all of the SAGE offices around the world.

The rest of the UK senior management team consists of a wider group of directors and associate directors, some of whom have been with the company for many years and others who have been brought in to bolster our skills in particular areas as we moved along. The current management structure in London includes three non-executive directors (Paul Chapman, Anne Farlow, and Brenda Gourley), four other directors (Phil Denvir, IT Director; Carol Irwin, HR Director; Clive Parry, Sales and Marketing Director; and Richard Fidczuk, Production Director), and Associate Directors Tony Histed, Jane Makoff, Miranda Nunhofer, Karen Phillips, Tessa Picknett, Richard Thame, and Leo Walford.

In India, we have Vivek Mehra as Managing Director of SAGE India, and as the founding Managing Director of our Asia-Pacific office, Steve Golden served from 2006 until early in 2010. The Asia-Pacific affiliate has its regional headquarters in Singapore and is incorporated in Singapore, but it has staff all around the region, including in Japan and in China. Today, we've got four sales staff in China, three in Beijing, and one in Shanghai, all working on selling our content into the Chinese market. We will be shortly recruiting staff under Asia-Pacific in Korea, Taiwan, and Australia as well.

A Sense of Community

Part of creating and sustaining a successful, international publishing company is creating and sustaining a successful, healthy workforce community. Publishing is a business that revolves around people—authors, customers, and employees. Empowerment—believing in people and trusting them to make decisions, to bring bright ideas, to fix problems—is critical at SAGE. Our employees are more than just workers; they are stakeholders in the decisions that affect the company. SAGE shares goals, progress, and financials every month in company-wide meetings that are a fundamental component of corporate community. Because relationships are important, feedback for management is provided by SAGE's Management Excellence Survey (MES) that is used throughout SAGE globally and is designed to provide those who manage two or more people the opportunity to receive performance feedback from their supervisor, peers, and reporting staff members.

This sense of a positive, supportive culture has grown to include the community in which SAGE is located and operates. In the best traditions of companies such as Ben & Jerry's or Patagonia, SAGE has striven in recent years to join a new generation of corporations that have a connection to their community and are responsible about the environment and sustainability—to succeed while still being unique, creative, and entrepreneurial and grow a business that gives back to the community.

The Human Resources department coordinates programs that connect employees to the community each year. In California, for example, we organize a food drive with MANNA (Metropolitan Area Neighborhood Nutrition Alliance) for people with acute life-threatening illnesses at Thanksgiving. We collect toys to be donated to Foy's Toys each December in time for the holidays. The employees personally and generously donate the food and the toys for these wonderful community programs.

The Books For Schools program, sponsored by SAGE, was established in 2007. In California, schools from Santa Barbara and Ventura Counties are invited to submit a grant application from their school library in order to receive a $1,000 cash grant to be used in purchasing books. Each school has to explain what books they would purchase with the money and why. Ten schools are selected annually to receive the grants. This was based on a program originated several years earlier by SAGE London.

Since the early 1990s, SAGE has been supporting the Conejo Valley Unified School District (CVUSD) in surrounding Ventura County. One of the programs SAGE supports is the International Baccalaureate (IB) program at Newbury Park High School, one of only 82 high schools statewide to offer this program. The program was initially begun in Europe to ascertain how much knowledge students had while crossing national boundaries and attending different schools. Students take internationally recognized advanced courses, including extensive research paper writing, and complete significant community service over a two-year period. The IB program concludes with a four-hour exam the students must pass in order to receive an IB diploma, recognized around the world at colleges and universities.

SAGE also supports annual language arts mini grants to schools for teachers within the district to strengthen their classroom programs. In addition, SAGE also provides funding for CVUSD teachers to attend summer writing programs such as the South Coast Writing Project at UCSB and the UCLA writing program. These summer programs help teachers to identify their own approaches to teaching writing, examine current theory and research in the teaching of writing, and write extensively in small groups to respond to each other's writing. Teachers are able to apply the lessons learned in these programs when they return to the classroom.

SAGE is currently supporting the Faculty Student Research Forum at California State University Channel Islands (CSUCI). CSUCI is the most recent addition to the California State University system and the only four-year public university in Ventura County. The Faculty Student Research Forum involves faculty and student teams in a multidisciplinary research experience, where students conduct original scholarly work under the mentorship of a full-time faculty member.

SAGE has also supported the Ventura County Office of Education with a grant that supports student competitions that promote world-class learning such as the Ventura County Academic Decathlon, the Ventura County Mock Trial, and the Ventura County Science Fair. Ventura County has consistently done well at these competitions, with Moorpark High School winning the national title in the Academic Decathlon for the third time and La Reina High School competing at the national level in the Mock Trial. Students from Ventura County schools continue to perform at high levels at the Science Fair, with many of them going on to the state level.

SAGE established the SAGE Scholarship, administered by the Ventura County Community Foundation, in 1995. Since that date, SAGE Scholarships have been awarded annually to college-bound high school graduates who have demonstrated their financial need and articulated their merit through a written essay. Students must demonstrate initiative and improvement in their academic accomplishments, as well as good citizenship.

SAGE has a Charity Matching Gift program for all employees. An employee can give up to $100 a year to the 501(c)(3) charity of his or her choice and SAGE will match the gift to the organization.

SAGE's philanthropic donations have also crossed international boundaries, with gifts in India commemorating various corporate milestones with donations to a variety of charities in Delhi and the annual fellowship awards to honor Tejeshwar Singh's memory that were announced in 2008 and early 2009.

Other charitable donations have been made in the United States commemorating the lives of former long-serving corporate outside directors connected with UC Berkeley and the University of Maryland.

Additional philanthropic activities include partnerships where SAGE joined the McCune family and in particular honored highly valued programs in higher education during recent years—many of them described in the following chapter.

The Greening of SAGE

This commitment to community means ensuring a clean, healthy environment by actively encouraging eco-friendly practices throughout our company, such as recycling, using recyclable packaging materials, and educating our employees on ways they can participate. Some green initiatives already implemented include organic teas and fair trade coffees; environment-friendly plasticware; areas for printer cartridge, cell phone, and battery disposal; and the elimination of plastic water bottles at Friday lunches.

Our new division acquired in 2008, Congressional Quarterly Press, has already implemented environmentally conscious initiatives, such as using 71% recycled paper, replacing lightbulbs with energy-efficient bulbs, and recycling plastic grocery bags. They also periodically hold an office cleanup and recycle day. Other initiatives being looked into are using solar panels, replacing urinals with waterless units, recycling sneakers, and identifying a local school for a partnership with Nike for a Green Fair. A book study group on Thomas L. Friedman's best-selling book, *Hot, Flat, and Crowded: Why We Need a Green Revolution and How It Can Renew America,* was recently formed and enjoyed by employees.

SAGE London and our other international affiliates have similar programs, each developed within a culturally and regionally appropriate framework.

CHAPTER 12

Toward Solutions

Miller-McCune *Magazine, the McCune Foundation, and Personal Philanthropy*

In my career as a publisher, I've seen quite an inspiring amount of research-based knowledge that could be directed toward real solutions for problems in our world today. Ever since 1965, SAGE Publications has been dedicated to the communication and dissemination of that knowledge within the global scholarly community, and now, especially in this first decade of the new millennium, I have sought to spread that commitment more widely. In doing this, I've been involved in two developments, one through the public media in the form of my magazine, *Miller-McCune,* and the other through philanthropic giving, supported by the McCune Foundation, SAGE-sponsored gifts, and my private donations to causes and projects I have been personally interested in.

Miller-McCune *Magazine*

A magazine to carry research-based knowledge beyond academia has always seemed to me like an effective way to reach more people in all walks of life and spheres of influence, especially those in positions to make major decisions of policy on national and international levels.

From the time we were children—George grew up in the Depression and I grew up in the aftermath of World War II—we were surrounded by social and political change. He was born in the roaring 1920's, but his earliest memories and life-forming experiences were of the Depression at its worst in Iowa and coastal Washington State. I was born in early 1941, but my earliest memories were of postwar events, first in my family and then in my community, and ultimately both in my country and the world as it was then.

I think we had different reasons for being politically conscious, but the important thing is that we were. We were also reasonably intelligent and well educated, and hoped that we could contribute in one way or another to making things better, at least for our families and communities, if not on a broader scope. I suppose, ultimately, people who are drawn to publishing, especially in the social and behavioral sciences, see social change and social justice as important goals to strive for—and see education as a means to reaching those goals.

Within two years of our autumn 1966 marriage, George and I were beginning to talk and think about such matters, not only between ourselves and to our few like-minded family members but also to our many like-minded authors and publishing colleagues.

We even consulted with (and twice attempted to buy) a magazine that had the potential of doing something similar to what we do today, although it was focused squarely in the social sciences and did not look at matters of the environment, science, and health science in a significant way that was rooted in scientific, medical, and technology research.

We also looked at and discussed acquisition or merger with two other social science magazines with somewhat similar focus to ours. I am not sure that any of them are still being published, although I think at least one is still alive somewhere in Europe with very little of an American sales or circulation presence.

Starting From Scratch, Again!

In 2007, the SAGE, Inc. Board encouraged me (after another failed attempt to purchase such a magazine) to start my own magazine from scratch. Money was allocated for a lean but reasonable 5-year budget, and the Miller-McCune

Center for Research, Media and Public Policy was formed as a separate non-profit to house the magazine, named *Miller-McCune*. The focus would be on environmental issues, health care, education, and the economy. I became the Center's President, and we started headhunting for the magazine's staff.

Geane DeLima, who started out at SAGE in 1991 as advertising manager for the journals division and rose to marketing director in her 13 years with the company, came back as a consultant and helped us with our early hiring. In September 2007, Geane became the Center's Executive Director. What a joy to work with her again!

The goal of the Center is to actively promote research in the social sciences aimed at finding solutions to stop or at least ameliorate some of the social problems we have in our world today. We felt that the available research is still very difficult to read and access, most of it in the form of journals kept at libraries. We also realized that certain subjects (such as health care or the environment) would require us to reach out to natural and physical scientists to present a comprehensive picture and realistic options for solutions. We wanted to make available new developments that are being published and released, and to write them up in a way that the general public, as well as public policy makers, could understand. We saw that we could use the print medium, which we're very familiar with, or we could do it online. We decided to do both.

At the outset, I knew we were taking a risk by launching a magazine when everyone was telling us it was a crazy idea, especially in tough economic times. But that kind of adversity hadn't stopped me in the past, when I began SAGE Publications in 1965 with just $500 and a one-room office in Manhattan. And so we went ahead.

Michael Todd, On-line Editor for the magazine, was hired in September, and John Mecklin, Editor-in-Chief, was hired in November, both coming to us from newspaper backgrounds. The first print issue of *Miller-McCune* appeared in April 2008. By the year's end, we had published six issues, and we are now appearing regularly on a bimonthly schedule in print. We grew very rapidly over the next year and a half, and today have a staff of eight full-timers and two fellows; we also have internships that guide developing journalists interested in policy solutions.

"It surprised me, how quickly we did it," Editor-in-Chief John Mecklin commented recently. "I expected it to be more of a two- to three- to four-year process, but we got a lot of notice very early. It's been a remarkably successful launch—almost everything that could have gone right has gone right."

When asked to what he attributes that success, John's own words express it best: "A lot has to do with the leadership and management style. Sara has high expectations and tends to pick people she thinks are good and supervises them in a way that works for talented people. She pays close attention without micro-managing people, giving them plenty of room, and even looks at every print version of M2 before it goes to press."

I think other factors have been at play in *Miller-McCune*'s success as well, especially the hard work of dedicated, smart people, and even the fact that we were launched in tough economic times, which helped to attract staff and freelance talent. Lots of entities were shutting down and laying off people at the time, and so we had less competition than had we started up in more prosperous times.

And of course, we did some innovative marketing. We did not aggressively market subscriptions as most new magazines do, but instead used a model of controlled circulation, sending out free copies to influential people. We probably have the same level of success and number of subscribers now as if we'd gotten out a huge direct mail campaign and blanketed the bookstores, but we thought that putting the magazine in people's hands was as good if not a better way of introducing it. Judging by its success, we were right. We do have paid subscribers, most of whom came to us through our Web site.

Another part of that success is attributable to sheer luck, such as when John Mecklin contacted James Fallows, a major figure in journalism, former Rhodes Scholar, author of many best-selling books, the main correspondent for the *Atlantic Monthly,* and former speech writer for President Carter. Fallows was asked if he would interview John when we launched, as a different way of announcing the magazine. Fallows didn't know John personally and was traveling in China at the time, but he agreed to do it, and the interview appeared in the first issue of the magazine.

We've continued to attract top-notch journalists as freelancers, such as Steve Weinberg, who was a long-time executive director of Investigators, Reporters and Editors, the main investigative reporting group in America, and author of several acclaimed books. Ryan Blitzstein, a less well-known journalist, who worked for *San Jose Mercury News* and *Red Herring Magazine,* writes regularly for *Miller-McCune* and is considered high-end in terms of writing and reporting.

Parts of the magazine and the online edition are also written by researchers, whose material gets edited until it reads the way good journalism reads, not in the style of an academic journal. In that sense, we're taking people who may or may not be well known in the research and academic fields and bringing them to this wider audience, which is a great benefit to them, but it's also an incredible benefit to our readers.

I'm always amazed at how interested people are in what our focus is, which is that we're empirical, driven by real research, not just by ideas. In the end, we want to employ that research to actively solve some of the pressing issues of the world, the nation, the family, the cities.

I've also been surprised at the willingness of many—not all, but many— academics and policy makers to take a chance and work with us. Sometimes SAGE's good name has helped, especially for the academics, but for the policy makers, SAGE and *Miller-McCune* are terra incognita. At one point, a writer was having difficulty getting a regulator who worked for an executive branch department in Washington, D.C., to return his phone calls. Then, we were picked up by the *Washington Post,* and the regulator called back immediately, mentioning he'd seen us in the *Post.* Although we don't need to be validated by the mainstream media, it's always very useful when we are.

Global Outreach Through the Web

The online edition of *Miller-McCune* magazine has also been hugely successful. All magazine stories ultimately get posted online at Miller-McCune.com, but we also generate a great deal of new content that appears only online. About 60% to 70% of the online material never goes into the print magazine, so in a sense the online version is a separate and much more comprehensive magazine.

Because our goal is to reach decision makers widely, it makes sense to use the Internet for a global and international reach. Most problems don't stop at a country's borders. If we have a climate issue, for example, that issue doesn't stop when we reach our country's border, so we need to have our answers transcend geopolitical boundaries. In addition, because the material is online, people who aren't policy makers but petition their congressional representative, senator, governor, or parliamentarian to make changes can have access to it.

Our online presence has grown tremendously, more than doubling in the volume of people who visit the site in just a year and a half. We're not all the way there yet, but we are definitely getting into the league of the best established of our peers. When we look to the *New Yorker* or *Atlantic Monthly,* which also have online content, we are clearly a new model that others are doing, and we are doing it well. (Compared with the *Wilson Quarterly,* which is very similar to what we do, our Web site traffic is about four times the amount they have.)

The online growth, as with the print medium growth, is largely due to stories being written in such a way that people can easily understand them. We try to be clear and direct, even adding a bit of fun, some joie de vivre, so people can enjoy reading the content and will read it in their leisure time.

One measure of our success is how many of our stories are being picked up by other media. Stories appearing in *Miller-McCune* and on Miller-McCune.com have been regularly linked to and commented on by a broad assortment of respected media organizations, including the *New York Times,* the *Financial Times,* the *Atlantic,* the *Washington Post,* Reuters, National Public Radio, *The Economist,* and *Harper's* magazine, among many others.

Again we're not looking for validation by other media, but we do get excited when other media sources, including those around the world, point to Miller-McCune.com in a way that says this is something worth reading.

At the close of 2009, we've been publishing two volumes during a little more than a year and a half and have already won several significant national journalism awards. Our combined readership, print and online, is over a quarter of a million. I am very pleased with our progress to date.

Articles That Make a Difference

Journalism influences leaders who change society, but proving that a particular news article caused a leader to support a specific policy initiative is a difficult and often impossible task. Leaders are human beings who have countless motives—honorable and base, conscious and not—and many sources of information. Still, it's clear that *Miller-McCune* magazine and Miller-McCune.com have had a significant impact, bringing new, research-based solutions to a wide audience of opinion leaders during the magazine's short two years of life.

These are a few examples of articles that have made an impact:

• *Miller-McCune* magazine received the Society of Environmental Journalists' (SEJ's) *Outstanding Explanatory Reporting Award* in the print medium in 2009, an award that is typically won by the *New York Times* or the *Los Angeles Times.* The award was for Valerie Brown's August 2008 story, "Environment Becomes Heredity." Contest judges said that Brown's "ability to break down the complicated scientific details surrounding how environmental impacts can affect future generations of animals was educational and entertaining—a rare combination in a story that dives into molecular biology, toxicology and genetics." Brown received her award at the SEJ annual conference in October 2009, which had a reported attendance of 600 journalists, governmental officials, and environmental experts from around the world, including former Vice President Al Gore, who gave the conference keynote address. During the conference, *Miller-McCune* magazine Editor-in-Chief John Mecklin spoke as part of a panel that included editors from *Discover, Scientific American,* and *Sierra* magazines.

• Contributing editor Ryan Blitstein's article, "Racism's Hidden Toll" (July/August 2009), gained widespread notice for its deft handling of University of Michigan professor Arline Geronimus's research showing that racism apparently causes black Americans to get sick and die younger than their white counterparts. The University of Maryland's Casey Journalism Center on Children and Families and the NAACP Legal and Educational Defense Fund both highlighted the story on their Web sites. The story was written about on more than a dozen Web logs, including the well-known *Huffington Post.* Bianca and Michael Alexander, California Broadcast Journalism Fellows at the University of Southern California/Annenberg School of Communication, were inspired by the story to travel to Michigan to interview Geronimus for a documentary on race and diabetes. "Racism's Hidden Toll" has shown up in at least one university syllabus (a psychology class at the University of Vermont), and it received unsolicited praise from researchers at the University of Pittsburgh and Harvard University, where a professor interviewed for the story says it was placed on academic e-mail list-servers related to race, health, and health disparities.

- The City University of New York's John Jay College Center on Media, Crime and Justice ("the nation's only practice-and-research-oriented think tank devoted to encouraging and developing high-quality reporting on criminal justice") invited *Miller-McCune* to enter its 2009 Excellence in Criminal Justice Reporting Awards. *Miller-McCune* contributor Steve Weinberg was subsequently cited as an honorable mention in the competition for his story "Innocent Until Reported Guilty" (October 2008), an in-depth look at how news media organizations can change their reporting methods to make it less likely that the innocent are sent to prison. The story was written about on the Web site of The Innocence Project, a national advocacy group founded by Barry Scheck and Peter Neufeld, which seeks to overturn wrongful convictions; the Legal Blog Watch at Law.com, the Web site for American Lawyer Media and its 20 national and regional legal publications; Simple Justice, a blog of the New York State Criminal Defense Bar; and Lawbeat, a blog by Mark Obbie, a journalism professor at the S.I. Newhouse School of Public Communications/Syracuse University and the former managing editor of *The American Lawyer* magazine.

- In "A History in the Making" (May/June 2009), *Miller-McCune* contributor Joan Melcher wrote about Julie Cajune, a teacher, curriculum designer, and member of the Confederated Salish-Kootenai Tribe, who is gathering the histories of Montana's 12 recognized tribes as part of a groundbreaking initiative to include American Indians in that state's history and educational system. A couple of months later, Melcher received a message from Cajune telling her that the Kellogg Foundation read her article in *Miller-McCune* and contacted her, saying her work fits with their grant priorities.

- The National Council on Crime and Delinquency gave one of its respected Prevention for a Safer Society (or PASS) Awards to *Miller-McCune* contributing editor Vince Beiser for his cover story "Is This the Future of the War on Drugs?" which looked at a Vancouver, B.C., program that aims to reduce the dangers attendant to drug addiction by providing addicts with drugs in a clinical setting.

- In 2009, the 133-year-old *Library Journal* ("the oldest and most respected publication covering the library field") and renowned magazine expert and University of Mississippi Journalism Department Chair Samir Husni (aka "Mr. Magazine") both placed *Miller-McCune* on their lists of best new magazines.

- In addition, the *Utne Reader* cited *Miller-McCune* for the best independent science and technology coverage in the country in 2008, putting the magazine in the category with MIT's *Tech Review* and other high-end science and technology magazines.

What is noteworthy about *Miller-McCune,* in both the online and print editions, is that talented, smart intellectuals and writers, both journalists and academic researchers, are coming together in a public forum on important issues in a way that is not dumbed down. The magazine is written so that any reasonably intelligent person can read it and enjoy it, not just academics or professionals in any narrow sense.

The Center's Vision and Activities

In addition to publishing the magazine, the Miller-McCune Center for Media, Research and Public Policy will also sponsor events that bring together people working on solutions, such as Town Hall, Los Angeles, a nonprofit, nonpartisan organization comprising leaders and engaged citizens dedicated to examining important issues facing our society. In November 2007, we sponsored Admiral David Brewer, 46th Superintendent of Los Angeles Unified School Districts, to present to Town Hall on the school district's annual "report card." We plan to do more such events in the future.

The long-term vision for *Miller-McCune* is to foster communication, so that people engage in dialogues with one another to learn from one another in a way that brings the communication full circle. Because important research often stops at universities, our aim is to get it out to the public and to the end user, the practitioners, the policy makers. Then they can begin to raise questions that get back to academics and scientists, further shaping research and solutions.

In our outreach, we are looking not only at the universities but also at foundations that are reporting initiatives and programs solving social and environmental issues. We invite them to share the results of the nonprofits or programs that they fund, further adding to the dialogue and knowledge dissemination. In the future, we plan to do events to bring journalists together along with influential policy makers and those in nonprofits and foundations, possibly starting in late 2010 or early 2011.

The McCune Foundation

My first foray into philanthropy began in 1990 when George and I created the McCune Foundation with the mission of doing work that had potential for a positive impact in the communities around the world where SAGE had its offices at that time. As I mentioned at the end of Chapter 10, this mission evolved over the decade and into the new millennium to focus on more local initiatives, specifically those in Ventura County, where SAGE has its offices, and in Santa Barbara County, where I live. Today, in addition to funding important social change, the McCune Foundation sponsors (through a personal contribution from me, backed up by a legacy gift in my estate plan) a Graduate Dissertation Fellowship at the UCSB Department of Communications in memory of the Foundation's co-founder and first President, my late husband, George D. McCune.

In 2001, the Foundation's Board of Directors shifted our focus to concentrate its funding in support of initiatives by community-based organizations that built "social capital," a concept that is still being defined and clarified by the organization. In a recent interview, Claudia Armann, the current Executive Director of the Foundation (which is now based in Ventura), gives the following definition (with the help of Marilyn Gittell, myself, and others who came together and worked hard at a recent Board retreat to arrive at consensus): "Social capital emerges when people work together around issues that matter to them and develop shared values and trust in their relationships. The bonds and alliances they form become what is referred to as 'social capital,' a kind of human resource that can be brought to bear and drawn upon when problems arise and people come together to find solutions."

In 2002, the McCune Foundation's Board of Directors agreed to sponsor a five-year program of grants to grassroots organizations with an emphasis on educational and other opportunities for the poor and underserved in nearby communities. This program was recently renewed for an additional period of five years. Today, we are especially interested in funding grassroots organizations that seek to empower the economically and politically disenfranchised—people without a voice—and encourage networking and coalition building within communities in Ventura and Santa Barbara.

The Foundation, starting with an annual contribution by SAGE of $500,000, began in 2001 to invest in initiatives that engaged community organizations to influence the decision-making process, which we believe is an essential part of making democracy work. In 2006, SAGE's contribution went up to $600,000, and it is slated to rise by $100,000 each year until 2010, when it will become $1 million and stay at that level. This will continue until shortly after my death (when the Foundation's endowment will be fully funded via a part of the family estate plan George and I outlined about a year before his death).

As of November 2009, the McCune Foundation's annual giving was $443,196 with an additional $75,000 pledged for two-year programs into November 2010. The following list of grantees from our most recent funding cycle, November 2009, is reflective of our interests:

Big Brothers Big Sisters of Ventura County, Inc.

$47,196 for One Step A La Vez, a youth committee to expand the voice for social change in Fillmore and Piru through grassroots activism, leadership, and community organizing

Central Coast Alliance United for a Sustainable Economy (CAUSE)

$50,000 per year for two years for general operating support for social, economic, and environmental justice programs focused on creating grass-roots power, policy reform, and systemic change in Ventura and Santa Barbara Counties

CAUSE (Arts for Action)

$30,000 to support operating expenses and capacity building for youth-based community organizing through the arts

CAUSE (Ventura County Clergy & Laity United for Economic Justice)

$50,000 in program support for a coalition of faith organizations advocating for immigration reform, farm worker housing, access to health care, and economic justice

Centro Binacional para el Desarrollo Indigena Oaxaqueño

$25,000 for Naa Xini 2 to enhance the Mixteco community's capacity to design and implement advocacy campaigns to solve social problems that affect Mixtecos and Latinos in Santa Maria

Coalition for Sustainable Transportation (COAST)

$40,000 for Alliance for Sustainable and Equitable Regional Transportation (ASERT) to provide operating support for a regional transportation alliance to promote public transportation and organize public activism among a diverse constituency of transit users

El Centrito Family Learning Centers

$30,000 for the Padres Promotores Education Project, which engages, trains, organizes, and empowers Oxnard parents to advocate for higher education for their children

Environmental Education Group, Inc. (Esperanza)

$25,000 to empower youth and families most affected by youth violence to advocate for a community-driven solution to youth violence prevention and to become actively engaged with local organizations and policy makers

La Hermandad Hank Lacayo Youth & Family Center

$25,000 for operating expenses for grassroots organizing and organizational leadership activities among working-class immigrants in Ventura County

Santa Barbara County Action Network
(University Park Mobile Homeowners Association)

$11,000 for organizing local mobile home residents and strengthening networks with statewide mobile home associations to protect homes from condo conversions and rent decontrol

Ventura County Community Foundation
(Social Justice Fund for Ventura County)

$25,000 per year for two years for capacity building, including an endowment drive for the Social Justice Fund and educational outreach to grassroots groups and donors

Second-Year Funding for Grants Awarded November 2008

Coalition for Sustainable Transportation (COAST)

$15,000 for capacity building through hiring of a part-time development director to secure new donors and new board members

Mixteco/Indigena Community Organizing Project

$35,000 for operating expenses, including staffing, to support community organizing work among indigenous Oaxacan farm workers in Ventura County

Santa Barbara County Action Network

$35,000 for operating and program expenses to support community organizing around social justice and environmental issues throughout Santa Barbara County

Social Venture Partners

In June 2009, I became a partner in a new chapter of a national movement in philanthropy known as the Social Venture Partners, Santa Barbara. SVPSB is currently a network of about 75 accomplished individuals who combine financial contributions and professional skills and creativity with a passion for impactful philanthropy. Together, our goal is to build a connection between entrepreneurial energy and grassroots innovation and make a hands-on difference in our region. Fundamental to the model is engagement: We work in partnership with nonprofits in the local communities to bring about positive social change. As partners, we have a wide range of experience in charitable giving, and together we decide how to leverage our pool of expertise and money to support collaborative solutions to social challenges.

SVPSB selected homelessness and the lack of transitional and low-income housing in Santa Barbara as its focus for current investments. The Partners expect to see change and betterment that lasts and transforms the organizations it invests in, as that organization benefits from expertise and skills in marketing, office functions, fundraising, and program/service delivery abilities. The dollar value of the investments in 2009 was $56,000, but the true impact of the investments will be made through the Partners' work as consultants with the selected organizations, valued at over $250,000.

The Social Venture Partners philanthropic model is gathering wide support in the United States, with chapters in more than 20 cities and regions as of the time this book was written. Our chapter has a current goal of both broadening the number of "partner units" (most are couples) and deepening our impact in Santa Barbara.

Other Philanthropic Investments (Corporate and Personal)

The long-standing tradition in many families of dropping coins into a metal box for weekly charity—in Hebrew called *tzdekah*—has blossomed into a larger enterprise with my other philanthropic efforts. Below, I list three separate categories of gift giving. The first is corporate gifts given by SAGE, Inc.

The second is gifts shared by me and SAGE, Inc., and a third are my personal gifts over time to my community.

Corporate Gifts

ALA (American Library Association): $15,000—This scholarship was created in memory of one of our board members, Peter Lyman, former university librarian and professor emeritus of the School of Information at the University of California, Berkeley. It is called the Peter Lyman Memorial/ SAGE Scholarship in New Media. It started in 2008 and is scheduled to go through 2012. It is administered by the American Library Association.

Brandeis/The Heller School: $227,500—The SAGE scholarship for Heller MBA students is offered to prepare students to lead organizations that are pursuing a social mission. This full-tuition scholarship opportunity is funded by SAGE for MBA students who demonstrate outstanding leadership potential, a commitment to managing for a social mission, and excellence in previous coursework. This scholarship program began in 2007 and expires in 2010.

KCLU (Radio Station at Cal-Lutheran University): $300,000—Since 1995, SAGE has matched gifts of its employees to the KCLU radio station. More recently, SAGE enabled the KCLU dream of purchasing a new signal in Santa Barbara County with a challenge grant to community listeners. The current pledge in place is intended for the purchase of a new radio station in Santa Barbara. This pledge began in 2009 and is scheduled to end in 2011.

McCune Foundation: $900,000—The focus of the McCune Foundation is supporting initiatives that offer practical assistance to community-based organizations in Santa Barbara and Ventura Counties. The Foundation is most concerned with supporting creative grassroots programs that focus on capacity building and social justice with a priority to fund projects creating a social or societal change, rather than individual empowerment or development of leadership skills in individuals. This pledge is renewed annually but will be capped at $1,000,000 per annum as of 2010.

Miller-McCune Center: $2,250,000—The Miller-McCune Center for Research, Media and Public Policy is a private operating foundation created to promote greater use of research results when addressing current and pressing social issues while seeking to fulfill its mission by demonstrating the quality and importance of social and scientific research and advancing the dissemination of research results in the media through its own publication(s), Web site, and internship programs. This pledge is renewed annually.

Santa Barbara Cottage Hospital: $2,500,000—This pledge is in support of The Campaign for Cottage Health System, the formal fundraising program to help build the new Santa Barbara Cottage Hospital. In recognition of this donation, Cottage will name the new medical library at the new hospital in SAGE's honor, which will serve not only Cottage physicians and staff but patients, students, medical researchers, and the community as well (this library is being constructed during the last phase of the building project in 2012–2013). This pledge ends in 2012.

Town Hall: $15,000—This pledge is for the Town Hall American Heritage Student Program with the purpose of bringing Los Angeles youth to Town Hall in order to hear directly from leaders in government, industry, culture, and science. This pledge began in 2007 and is renewed annually.

UCSB SAGE Center for the Study of the Mind: $2,500,000—This gift was made to commemorate the SAGE 40th Anniversary and to launch a dynamic new interdisciplinary research center for the study of the mind, bringing together UC Santa Barbara scholars from a broad range of academic disciplines in the arts and humanities, social sciences, the sciences, and engineering to explore the multidimensional nature of the human mind. This pledge will be completed in 2010. Annual operating support funds for the Director's initiatives have begun and are eligible for modest renewal sums.

UCSB Visiting Scholar Accommodations for SAGE Center: $1,000,000—This pledge has brought the foremost researchers to UCSB to study the brain and the mind, as well as to participate in seminars and conferences. This pledge ends in 2010.

UCSB SAGE Center Executive Director: $150,000—This pledge is an additional gift that has been made on an annual basis to be spent at the discretion of the Center's Founder and Executive Director.

UCSB SAGE Center Housing: $72,000—This pledge covers visiting scholar housing. This pledge ends in 2010.

UNT (University of North Texas): $5,000—This pledge is an annual sponsorship for the UNT Emerald Ball, which is in support of the Emerald Eagle Scholars. This program was created for students who are academically talented, as shown by their admission acceptance into UNT, who have an average freshman class SAT score of 1,105. Qualifying students will also have limited financial resources, making it difficult to fulfill their dreams of a university education. This pledge is eligible for annual renewal.

Shared Gifts (SAGE, Inc. and SMM)

AAPSS (American Academy of Political and Social Science): $25,000—This was a challenge grant for the Daniel Patrick Moynihan Prize Fund that consisted of matching funds from SAGE and Sara Miller McCune. It is a two-year commitment that began in 2008. The Daniel Patrick Moynihan Prize fund honors social scientists and public officials who have distinguished themselves in using social science to advance the public good.

CAMA (Community Arts Music Association): $1,500,000—This pledge is intended to help CAMA continue to bring world-class orchestras and soloists to perform in Santa Barbara through CAMA's Orchestra Series, which was relocated to the newly renovated Granada Theatre in the 2008–2009 concert season. This pledge began in 2007 and is scheduled to go through 2011. With this partnership, SAGE receives recognition at sponsored events and a limited number of tickets to each concert that are raffled off to employees for the benefit of the SAGE Scholarship Fund.

Center for Advanced Study in the Behavioral Sciences: $1,500,000—This pledge is in support of the Center's work of improving contributions of the social and behavioral sciences and humanities by facilitating interdisciplinary perspectives, depth of inquiry, integration of knowledge, and application to real-world concerns. This pledge began in 2008 and ends in 2012. The Center is adjacent to the Stanford University campus. The Center is also the beneficiary of an irrevocable legacy bequest in the McCune Estate Plan.

Samuels Center: A bit over $50,000 (with me adding the balance to bring the total amount to $80,000 per annum). This pledge is in honor of dear friends of Sara Miller McCune and SAGE, Irwin and Marilyn Gittell. The Gittells' association with SAGE began in the mid-1960s, with Irwin being the Company's first accountant, and his wife, Marilyn, the founding editor of one of the Company's bestselling journals, *Urban Affairs Quarterly* (now *Urban Affairs Review*). Marilyn built the Samuels Center for the Study of State and Local Government at the CUNY Graduate Center—near the New York City Public Library. The Graduate Center provides doctoral education of the highest quality for many of the nation's brightest and most intellectually ambitious men and women. This grant makes it possible to build upon this tradition of excellence and helps share the benefits of outstanding scholarship with the greater community. This pledge ends in 2010. Sadly, Professor Gittell died in February 2010.

Personal Gifts to the Community

The gifts listed below are eclectic (as are my interests). They are representative of current annual giving commitments, although in many cases I have been committed to these causes for a decade or even more. Most are paid and/or receive appropriate annual or topical gifts dependent on their current campaigns. Some will also receive legacy gifts.

- University of California at Santa Barbara to establish an endowed chair for the Dean of Social Sciences—currently Dean Melvin Oliver
- Santa Barbara Center for the Performing Arts (Granada Restoration Project)
- UCSB Arts & Lectures
- UCSB Foundation (Mosher Alumni House/Rose Miller Terrace)

- Walter H. Capps Center for the Study of Ethics, Religion and Public Life (UCSB)
- Hillel (UCSB)
- Fielding Graduate University
- La Casa de Maria
- New Beginnings
- Fund for Santa Barbara
- Congregation B'nai B'rith
- Santa Barbara Maritime Museum
- Serenity House
- Opera Santa Barbara
- Santa Barbara Bowl
- Food Bank of Santa Barbara County
- Santa Barbara Symphony
- Anti-Defamation League
- Human Rights Watch
- The Jewish Federation
- Santa Barbara Foundation
- B'nai B'rith Youth Organization
- Rehabilitation Institute (now a part of Cottage Hospital, Santa Barbara)

CHAPTER 13

Family and Friends

A history of SAGE would not be complete without mention of the role played by family in the company—and in my life. By family, I mean specifically members of both George's and my families, as well as the networks of families we were drawn into by the nature of our business—and those we drew into our own family. These bonds have been the source of much delight and friendship over the years, providing me with great sustenance and joy. Individually and together, they have contributed some of my most precious memories.

Family has always been very important to me, and since SAGE has also been important, the two have often become intertwined. In a recent interview, I was asked if I'd originally envisioned SAGE as a family business when I started out back in 1965. My answer was and is "no." I was not thinking of a family business at the time, although a year and a half after I began the company, I married George (in October 1966), and we built the company together until his death in May 1990.

I still don't think of SAGE as a family business, given that there are more than 1,000 employees in offices across four continents. But family is linked to the enterprise, beginning with the fact that I had come from a family of entrepreneurs (my dad and his brothers each had businesses of their own). After I'd incorporated, they helped me by loaning me some start-up capital, but no one in my family had any publishing experience. (See more about early family connections in Chapter 1.)

Once George and I were married, running the business became truly a family affair. Most of our business decisions were made jointly, such as whether to publish in a new area or to raise money from outside (from venture capitalists, bankers, individual investors, whatever). We both agreed that we never wanted to go public but would remain a closely held family business. Furthermore, we did not differentiate between the office and home. We brought many authors to our home to discuss concepts and issues, sometimes working long into the wee hours of the morning at our home as well as our office in Southern California. After we acquired our first home, a cabin in Yosemite, we would occasionally "kidnap" our authors if they were well past their deadlines and bring them to that secluded location to finish major projects, so that we could go to press. We were so in tune with our authors on the personal and intellectual levels that we were often able to help them through "writer's block" and keep them focused.

George's children, and my stepchildren by marriage, were never outright encouraged to join the business, yet all four of them—and three of our four grandchildren—have worked in one capacity or another at the company over the years. They are all talented individuals in their own right, and earned their positions by interviewing and being qualified, just as any other employee might.

David F. McCune had the longest and most significant tenure, first as Vice President for two years and then, having been promoted nine months before George died, as President for nine more years (1988–1998). Before that, he consulted for SAGE, Inc., and I must give him credit for being the person who first taught me how to use a Compaq computer while consulting for us for a week or so during 1978. (In those days, a Compaq weighed 25 pounds and was encased in metal—hardly a very portable device!) For years, George relied on me heavily for my limited computer skills (especially when we were together at our home in Yosemite), since he had never learned how to use a computer himself. I think at first he was still extolling the marvels of other new gizmos; then there were health issues, and subsequently there were time issues.

As a young man, David lived in Sweden where he worked on an experimental dairy farm, and ultimately (after graduating from Williams College) he moved back to southern Sweden for several years. While there, he attended journalism school, and earned a living as a journalist in Sweden (also doing some freelance journalism in Germany). He subsequently returned to the United States and joined the staff of Time, Inc. David's first wife, Susan, was like a sister to me and died of cancer in 1999, at a very early age. About four years later, David remarried at a three-day wedding festival in Sweden. His beautiful wife is Gunilla Lavén, whom we call Nilla. They spend half the year in Sweden and half the year in California, and today David serves on SAGE's Board of Directors and as Chairman of its Finance Committee.

Cathy Sarvat Ohlson is David's sister, older by 15 months, and is married to Tom Ohlson. Cathy lives in Jamison, Pennsylvania, part of Bucks County, where she is a retired public school teacher who taught gifted children for 31 years. Even though retired, she still keeps her hand in the business of learning by working in a Borders bookstore. When Cathy was in college (she is a graduate of Temple University), she would come out to California for the summer and work in the SAGE offices, living with us or renting an apartment with a friend. Today Cathy is the mother to three of our four grandchildren: Samantha Sarvat, Ashley Horne, and Richard Sage Sarvat.

Susan McCune Trumble is the youngest of my four stepchildren. She is married to Lee Trumble, and they have two sons from his prior marriage. Susan worked for Regis Corporation, a leader in the hair care industry, in a variety of management positions for 20 years (1983–2003), including as a technical educator for their Southern California Supercuts locations. In 1995, Susan relocated to New York to support the company's expansion and served in roles ranging from recruitment and retention director, new franchisee liaison, and finally, corporate management trainer for the Eastern region of the United States and Canada. In 2001, Susan returned to California, adding Regis's Western region to her continued role in supporting their Metropolitan New York market. From 2003 to 2009, Susan owned and operated a fitness franchise in Malibu, California, and in 2009, she brought her knowledge and skills to SAGE Publications, joining the Organizational Development Department in her role of designing and delivering in-house learning initiatives, with the majority of programs specifically designed for management learning.

Keith McCune, the second youngest of my four stepchildren, worked for SAGE, Inc. when we were a smaller company, and also worked at SAGE London for a while in order processing and in the warehouse. He is very intelligent and personable, but he has had some health issues over the years and has not pursued a career because of his health.

At different times while they were growing up, our younger children lived with George and me in California. We helped raise Keith first, and then after he moved out, Susan lived with us for at least two years. We had custody of Keith and Susan during the summertime.

I first met Cathy and David as youngsters, about ages 11 and 9, respectively, when George had them in New York City for part of their summer vacation. I didn't see them again until Cathy came out for summer jobs at SAGE while she was in college. David told a moving story about his reunion with George as an adult at George's memorial service, describing how they met again in Scandinavia after not having seen one another for many years. I remember that trip vividly—meeting David in Copenhagen, traveling by ferry to Sweden and then by car and rail to Norway.

David also joined us shortly thereafter on a business trip to London, and his relationship with the family has grown stronger over the decades in multiple ways.

From the late 1960s through the 1980s, we would often have house-guests who would dine with us, and the younger children joined us until they became bored if we talked too much business, and would ask to be excused. I remember Susan's reaction to Morris Janowitz—*Can anyone be that old?* She was maybe six years old when Molefi Asante, the founding editor of the *Journal of Black Studies,* and his wife came to dinner. I don't think she'd actually sat down at a table with someone not of her own race up to that point. She had lived in a part of Queens, New York, that was an enclave of first and second generations from Czechoslovakia, and I think her mother, Olga, was protective of both her son, Keith, and her daughter, Susan, especially before they all moved to California.

Susan and Keith were a little older when F. Gerald (Jerry) Kline came to our home in Beverly Hills and decided to cook us all a fresh seafood dinner. Jerry prepared a huge pot of water, leaving it over a low flame, and then went to Santa Monica where he picked up a live lobster and two large crabs. When he arrived back at our house, he turned the heat back up to boil, and then put the flailing bodies into the boiling water as the children watched. Susan was horrified and couldn't eat a bite, while Keith made his own dinner of Pepsi and potato chips. Jerry was a great chef, and as Dean of the School of Journalism for the University of Minnesota, his recipe for homemade bread was published in the newspaper to the great delight of his wife and four sons (not to mention the faculty, and the many authors he had lured to SAGE)!

The two younger children grew up knowing me with a bulging briefcase during the summers, while George was often working late at the office in Beverly Hills, and I would take them to the park after day camp. They also remember authors frequenting our home a few blocks away in West Los Angeles, engaged in conversations about their work and fields. I think it was very different from when they lived with their mother, Olga, who had moved nearby in Hollywood when the children were ten and six. Olga died when Susan was a young adult, a few years after George died. David and Cathy's mother died a few years after that, around 1995. Currently, I'm the only parent left standing.

The Grandchildren

The four grandchildren, Samantha, Doug, Ashley, and Sage, have all been very important to me. I remember George making me promise that I would take care of them if anything ever happened to him. Here they are, in order of birth:

Samantha Sarvat is the oldest of Cathy's three children from her prior marriage. Not quite a year older than Doug, Samantha resides in Lambertville, New Jersey, with her boyfriend, Erik Povisils, and works in Bucks County as an office manager for a construction supply company. After earning an Associate Degree in Hotel & Restaurant Management from Bucks County Community College, she has worked as a manager in both the retail and hotel industries. Samantha enjoys music tremendously and, in the past, has spent much of her spare time as a booking agent for both local and international musicians, a hobby at which she excels. Like her mother, Samantha spent a summer working at SAGE, Ltd in London doing both office and warehouse work.

Douglas D. McCune is the son of David and his first wife, Susan Watt. Like David, Doug is also currently on our Board of Directors. He is a graduate (class of 2004) of Stanford University. Family members are not invited to be on the Board of Directors unless they can contribute to the business; Doug is a software engineer, currently developing Web applications for data visualization, and so was invited to serve because of his talent, knowledge, and expertise in the field of technology. Doug is engaged to be married to a lovely young lady, Jocelyn Sze, whom he met while they were both attending Stanford. Jocelyn is currently completing her dissertation work at UC Berkeley (in the field of clinical psychology), and they will be married in the Stanford University Chapel in the summer of 2010.

Ashley Horne is Cathy's middle child, married to Edward Horne. They have three adorable boys; Gabe (Gabriel) is the oldest, Eli (Elijah) is the second, and the newest, born in September 2009, is Jax, short for Jakob Alexander. Ashley is a graduate of Chatham University, where she received a scholarship and also earned her MBA degree. She has spent the past two years working as an HR generalist and recruiter for a plastics manufacturer outside of Pittsburgh, Pennsylvania. The last time I visited Ashley and her family, Eli had just been born and Gabe was a little over three. I was teaching Gabe how to flip coins, when pretty soon he had won all my quarters and was about to take my last nickel, before being carried off to bath and bed. I didn't go totally broke, but it was close!

Richard Sage Sarvat, Cathy's youngest, is named after myself and George. Sage was born about six months after George died. Sage lives with his mother and stepfather in Bucks County, Pennsylvania, and works as a carpenter's assistant. Sage, like his sister Samantha, has a gift for working with his hands. He enjoys woodworking and mechanics. He also has shown a passion for physical fitness and nutrition, and likes to pass his knowledge on to those willing to listen. Sage is gentle, funny, and loyal, and has developed in stature to be much like his grandfather.

When the three oldest grandchildren—Samantha, Doug, and Ashley—were of an age, I arranged with their parents to have them travel with me (usually they were between the ages of 14 and 18 when we did this). I would take each of them with me to England on one of my summer trips. (Sage, the youngest, grew up in a period when I wasn't healthy enough to travel much, so we're still working on that.) We also arranged to have each grandchild take a trip with me (in the United States or Canada) that they chose separately, during their teenage years.

Samantha picked Western Canada, so I flew with her to Winnipeg, and we traveled by car into British Columbia. We took a side trip north from Lake Louise and had a close encounter with a moose late at night on an eight-lane highway that I don't think either of us will ever forget! Doug picked

Washington, D.C., starting with a helicopter tour from Reagan Airport. Ashley also picked D.C., and Sage is planning another trip to California (hopefully to Santa Barbara, this time). They've all been to Yosemite and stayed at our cabin in Wawona at the southern end of the park. One memory is of going with Cathy and her kids when they were young on a gold digging tour in the hills beyond Yosemite to pan for gold—my fingers almost fell off because the water was so cold, but the kids loved it.

Our travels were always educational, a high value in our family and in our business, and we always offered a menu of activities for the day in the different locations. I remember when Samantha and I went to Western Canada, we took in a performance of *Romeo and Juliet,* which was the first time she had enjoyed an encounter with Shakespeare. Then, when it was Sam's turn in London, we managed to squeeze in a side trip to Dublin with me and a couple of girl pals to see *A Midsummer Night's Dream.* I took Doug to many shows in London, and we also managed to catch some theater in Washington, D.C., where once we saw a performance of *Hamlet* one night and a farce about hairdressers another evening at the John F. Kennedy Center for the Performing Arts. Doug also liked to go to the museums and view famous documents, such as the Constitution and the Declaration of Independence. Ashley was fascinated with the National Museum of African Art and Smithsonian Institution, and we made two trips there during our brief trip to D.C. together.

Another thing I did with our grandchildren for a number of years, based on an idea of Jerry Kaplan's, was to give them each a certain amount of money once a year that they could contribute to a charity of their choice. This turned out to be an important and valued tradition. I still see the grandchildren now that they are older, but Ashley, Samantha, and Sage all live in the Northeast, and so our meetings are less frequent. Doug, of course, I see more often, due to his current connection to SAGE, and also because he lives in California.

George's and My Parents

Susan and Keith got to know George's parents, Esther and Jim McCune, who were quite hearty into their old age, and visited them at their place in the desert after they retired. It was near Parker, Arizona, part of a complex developed on land leased from the Colorado River Indian Tribe on the border between California and Arizona. George had four living siblings, two older and one younger. His oldest sibling was his sister, Mary. Bob Gouvion (Mary's husband) and their three boys were probably the closest to us of George's siblings. We were fortunate to have one of their sons (John Gouvion) working for us when the company was quite small.

I remember putting together a dinner for George's parents' 50th wedding anniversary with the siblings and their spouses at the Lawrence Welk dinner and theater complex out in the California desert. Lawrence Welk himself came over to our table and played the "Anniversary Waltz" to Esther and Jim on his accordion, and then Mr. Welk rushed off to watch himself on TV while George's mom cried happily and Jim blushed. For George's parents' 55th wedding anniversary, we had a party in our home in West L.A. (near the office in Beverly Hills), gathering all of the siblings and spouses, plus all the grandchildren we could round up: cousins, nieces, and nephews. This was before 1990, and I didn't think our flat, which was only the ground floor of a duplex, could get that many people crammed into it. But we did it buffet style, and everyone was very thrilled to be at such a momentous occasion.

My parents, Rose and Nathan ("Nat") Miller, would visit us frequently when we were first married. Usually we put them to work part of the time, but we also managed to show them as much as we could of California, including one memorable trip to San Francisco. On some occasions, after my dad's death, my mother would travel with us, and on one visit to London to celebrate Susan's 16th birthday, she came along to be Susan's chaperone. They would plan their day around theater and/or sightseeing, and during that particular visit, Mother took Susan to see the Agatha Christie play that ran for about 50 years (*The Mousetrap*). My mother was great to have along, although I think on that trip, she and Susan drove George a little crazy once or twice. We also had a lot of fun together after work (with theater in the evenings, a weekend trip to Chester, and visits to several nice restaurants, where Susan's blonde beauty and my mom's infectious laugh made the staff extra attentive).

My Aunt Adele (known to us all as "Dell") is also one of my closest friends. My mother's generation consisted of five girls and one boy (Dell's fraternal twin Marty). Sadly, these days, only Dell and her next older sister, Evelyn, are still with us. Both sisters live in North Carolina, but we are working on Dell (and her daughter, my cousin Judith Feierstein) moving to the Denver area.

This will give us a better chance to party together, plan and take trips together, and generally have fun. Dell will continue to visit her son Steve and his family on the East Coast, but Steve and Lisa usually visit me at least once a year, and their boys will both be in college next year, so there will be plenty of opportunity for family and friends to get together on both the East and West Coasts. Dell is also a very talented artist, and I think she will enjoy new scenery to sketch.

I see my brother, Avi, less frequently now, since he moved to Israel in 1984. Occasionally he arranges to take part of his summer vacation in either London or California. And of course we stay in touch by telephone. But I haven't visited him in Jerusalem for many years.

My Extended Family of Friends

There are so many friends who have been like family members to me—either because they became part of my family, or I was taken into their families—creating a wide network that endures to this day.

I am lucky to have a close friend from my college days, Margaret Sirot. Marge and I met in a freshman English class and knew we would be friends. Then she went out of town for another two years of college before returning to graduate from Queens College the same time I did (June 1961). We worked together on the senior yearbook (I was Editor, she was second in command) did quite a bit of double-dating, and her first husband (Marv Sirot) and George were very close friends. Marge always claimed that they communicated with short grunts and always understood exactly what was being said in the fewest possible words (or sounds). Her children, Ellen, Amy, Adam, and Laura (and their spouses and children), are all a part of my family, and I am a part of theirs.

I consider Matt Jackson, his wife Marian, their two sons (Paul and David), and their grandchildren to be part of my family, having known Matt and Marian since my earliest days at Pergamon in Oxford (see Chapter 4). I make it a point to always have dinner with them when I am in London, where they now live in Elstree (a suburb of London). We share a love of live theater and have been to countless productions together. If I guessed two hundred, I don't think I would be far off! Often when I visit the UK, we arrange to combine visits with Paul at Elstree or in London, and one or more of his children will join me and their grandparents for dinner or theater. Nikki and David

Jackson's kids are younger, so we tend to see each other around family cele-
brations, holiday meals, or that wonderful British institution, teatime!

Eric Buckley was a friend I stayed in touch with from my days of working in
Oxford. I knew his first wife, Joan, from my time working at Pergamon. After
Joan died, George and I stayed in touch with Eric and saw him several times a
year. Eric continued to serve on various boards and was a consultant to a number
of publishers after he retired from Pergamon. I remember visiting him after he
remarried; his second wife was an American scholar with a great sense of humor
and a delightful Southern accent; she taught a course during summer sessions at
Oxford University and also served as the book review editor for a major
Shakespeare journal. I remember one time going punting with Eric on a river in
Oxford, accompanied by my granddaughter Ashley. Eric was also good about
turning up at various SAGE parties. I guess the last time I saw him was at our 40th
anniversary celebration in London in the summer of 2005.

Another close friend from my year at Pergamon is Manu Roy Chakravarty.
Manu was working in England while her fiancé, Gautham Chakravarty, took his
second degree at Oxford University. Manu's second job in the UK was working
for me at Pergamon. Gautham was part of a small group of friends (including
Sunil Sinha and his fiancée, Loni) who were also doing second (or third) degrees
at Oxford. Somehow we all became buddies (Manu actually lived in the same
building I did during my stay in Oxford, while Gautham was in digs at his college). Manu and Gautham now live in Hawaii most of the year but visit India to
see family annually. Their children (daughter Shona and her husband Andy
Tepper, and son Rahul) and their grandchildren are another limb on my family
tree (along with Manu's brothers and sisters in India and their offspring, and
Gautham's sister and mother in Calcutta/Kolkatta). The Sinhas live in San Diego
where Sunil (Sonny) is on the physics faculty at UCSD. He and Loni still keep in
touch with me by phone. The Chakravartys and I visit wherever we can manage
to meet up (Hawaii, India, California, NYC), and Manu, Margaret, and I still try to
fit in a monthly joint phone call when we are all in the United States!

Marilyn Gittell was my political science teacher and college mentor. Until
her death in February 2010, she was doing research on cities and urban economic development, especially as it relates to the poor and underserved, at
the City University of New York Graduate School. There she taught a graduate
course and was the Director of the Samuels Center. We served on two boards
together (the McCune Foundation and the Samuels Center). Her son, Ross
Gittell, is a college professor (as is his wife, Jodi), and her daughter (Amy) is a

medical doctor, married to another M.D. Marilyn and I kept each other posted on the exploits of our various offspring. For several years, after being widowed, we both enjoyed travel, good theater, nice restaurants, and fine wine together.

Sandra Ball-Rokeach and I have known each other since 1986, when she and her late husband (social psychologist Milton Rokeach) moved from Pullman, Washington, to the University of Southern California (USC). Sandra is still teaching and doing research at the Annenberg School at USC. She also serves on the Board of the McCune Foundation (as do David McCune and Susan McCune Trumble). Sandra and I meet in L.A. or Santa Barbara or Yosemite, these days with our respective dogs, Jennie and Duke. Sandra and George really share a lot of characteristics: ethical values, respect for individuals of all colors and creeds, a sense of beauty, especially as seen and experienced in natural surroundings. And I think Sandra and I share not only these things but also a sense of how powerful and important family members are to our lives.

This is something that is probably characteristic of all my friendships as I have grown to adulthood. It certainly explains why George and I felt so strongly about two other families who are still very much part of my life today: John and Mary Wiemann and Howard and Jane Giles.

The Wiemanns first met George at an International Communication Association (ICA) convention shortly after John received his Ph.D. I was at another convention in another city (that was the story of our lives for a number of years). The ICA was an interesting and intellectually dynamic organization that brought together scholars in diverse fields of communication studies. John and Mary were researching and publishing on interpersonal communication. John, later in his career, moved into university administration and retired this past summer (2009) from his position as Vice Chancellor for Institutional Advancement at UCSB. Mary retired a year earlier from Santa Barbara City College, where she was department chair.

John and Mary are part of my extended family—I often spend part of Christmas or part of Thanksgiving with them, and we cross paths and visit with each other in places like Yosemite (as well as Santa Barbara). I knew their two children, Johnnie and Mollie, from the time they were quite young. Now they are both married, following lively careers. Johnnie is an M.D. and newly wed to Andrea. Chad and Mollie have a young son, William, who likes my dog, Duke, and loves his own dog, the much larger Otis.

The Wiemanns were incredibly supportive when I was widowed in 1990 and decided to move to Santa Barbara. They housed me on my home-hunting expeditions, which started two years after George's death. (Because we had friends in L.A. as well as Santa Barbara, I confined my searches for a new home to those two areas.) It was also interesting to be a part of their careers. Between the two of them, they've faced so many deadlines from me that they were happy to know I, too, had a deadline in writing this book on the history of SAGE. I can hear them saying, *Oh, good! Now Sara has to learn some deadline discipline!*

Howard (aka "H" or Howie) and Jane Giles and I have known each other from our Bristol days (1979). Now at the University of California, Santa Barbara, Howie was originally known and respected as a social psychologist in the UK. (In fact, he was the first, youngest, and only Chair in that department at the University of Bristol—in British universities, at that time, there was only one Chair in a department). Howie did not know George well, but we can literally say that I have known their son Robbie since birth. Jane was pregnant with Robbie when George and I first visited the lovely Giles home in Santa Barbara—not so coincidentally, across the street from where John and Mary Wiemann live. Robbie is now at Emory University. I guess time does fly when you are having fun! The Giles' lovely back garden (known as "Greece" for its resemblance to its namesake) has been the site of many a party for communication scholars from near and far. We have also managed to have good times in other venues, including London and Yosemite.

Howie's tribute in *A Celebration in Words: SAGE 1965–2005* expresses that association beautifully:

A Celebration in Words: SAGE 1965–2005
Howard Giles, *University of California, Santa Barbara*

SAGE helped me become what some referred to as a "cultural traitor" and settle away from British social psychology at the University of California, Santa Barbara (UCSB), in the Communication Department. Sara McCune, who became a close friend and confidante, assisted in this process, and I have edited two SAGE journals as well as a book series. I met George only a couple of times, although the sentiments expressed about this celebrated man at his Memorial in the Malibu Hills have always lived with me.

In the late 1960s–1970s, SAGE was the sponsor of important journals and serials for the emergent discipline of communication, itself an interdiscipline. Consensus is, amongst the historical leaders of the International Communication Association, that many foundations of the discipline were built from the pages of SAGE Publications, which so insightfully and generously supported its practices. Hence, in what turned out to be the first International Conference on Language and Social Psychology at Bristol, England, in the summer of 1979, we enquired of SAGE whether they would stand by us in this unpredictable project. Gratifyingly, they did!

There are so many individuals like myself and family, research fields, disciplines, professional associations, universities, and cities who are forever enriched because of Sara's attentions. We are especially blessed to share in her and SAGE's incredible accomplishments in being an acknowledged world leader in publishing the social sciences after 40 devoted years.

Sander Vanocur, a friend of Pat Moynihan's and a broadcaster for NBC's television news during the latter part of World War II, now lives here in Montecito. He and I have served on a committee at UCSB for the Communication Department. I value Sandy's judgment and thoughts highly, and he and his wife Ginny cross paths with me a few times a year. He is almost exactly George's age. Sandy still visits Liz Moynihan whenever he goes back to New York, and through him, as well as the American Academy for the Political and Social Sciences, I've gotten to know Liz (Pat's widow) and Maura, their daughter.

Judi and Harry Wiesbart are close friends and fellow residents of Santa Barbara, where I moved to my present home in the fall of 1992. Judi accompanied me and Kate Wilde on our 2009 trip to India and made a book of magnificent photographs to commemorate the visit. One of her photos appears in this volume.

Léni Fé Bland is a close friend and greatly admired philanthropist who lives in Montecito, California. She has been a Chartered Accountant in the UK; has lived in England, France, and Switzerland; and is fluent in two languages and comfortable in at least two others. Leni has served on the Board of the Santa Barbara Center for the Performing Arts and Santa Barbara's Music Academy of the West, and is currently on the board of the Community Arts Music Association, which brings great orchestral performances to the Santa Barbara community throughout the year. She is also a member of the Board of Directors for the Miller-McCune Center for Research, Media and Public Policy.

CHAPTER 14

Who Knows What the Future Will Hold?

To accomplish great things, we must not only act, but also dream; not only plan, but also believe.

—Anatole France

Those words have wisdom for the present as well as the past, and in as many ways as possible, I have tried to live by such wisdom. Certainly dreaming and believing have played a huge role in the plans and actions that grew SAGE Publications over the past 45 years.

Back in 1965, when we were first getting off the ground, George's worst fear was that no one with a solid reputation would believe in us enough to publish with us. However, that fear was allayed within the first two years of SAGE's existence. We were astonished, touched, and ultimately challenged by how much our authors trusted and believed in us.

We, in turn, could *not* let them down. They needed us—and need us now more than ever—in order to communicate with their colleagues, with policy makers, and foundations, and to form the kinds of networks that help academics and researchers achieve their goals with regard to desirable social change. Such access allows our authors to tweak public policy and enter into the debate of how scarce public monies might best be spent. We believed that those who publish with us richly deserve such a forum.

In our first 30 years, the dream George and I had of expansion and worldwide reach was more than realized. Then, beginning in 1995, I began to nurture another long-held dream. I took on several philanthropic responsibilities, primarily with the McCune Foundation and the Foundation Board of Trustees for the University of California at Santa Barbara. I also served on the board at the Fielding Graduate University for eight eventful years (including a year as interim President, which coincided with being Chair of their Board of Trustees).

During that period, for about 12 years, I was active with a local project to restore the historic Granada Theatre, where I served as Chief Financial Officer and Chair of the Capital Campaign Committee as a Board member of the Santa Barbara Center for the Performing Arts (SBCPA). I resigned from the SBCPA Board in June 2008, four months after the Granada restoration was reopened to great acclaim. At the end of 2009, I also left the UCSB Foundation Board to devote more time to other projects. I currently serve as Executive Chairman of SAGE Publications, Inc.; President and Publisher of the Miller-McCune Center for Research, Media and Public Policy; President of the McCune Foundation; Director (i.e., board member) of SAGE Publications, Ltd (SAGE London); and a member of the Board of Directors for the American Academy of Political and Social Science (which is headquartered in Philadelphia).

Contributing to Humanity

I deeply believe in the words of Rabbi Hillel, the Jewish scholar and theologian, spoken more than 2,000 years ago: *If I am not for myself, who will be for me? If I am not for others, what am I? And if not now, when?* These words have inspired me to become increasingly involved in identifying and hopefully shaping the resolution of some of the world's most extensive and demanding problems.

Today we live in a world where there is great wealth and great poverty. I have been troubled by that situation, because such conditions challenge my beliefs about informing the world of the social issues and problems we are facing and about possible solutions. I am committed to seeing programs started that attempt to resolve these issues and then evaluate their results, letting others know the next generation of solutions. My late friend Donald Campbell, an extraordinary social scientist and one of the founding fathers of the field of evaluation studies, believed in that approach, and so do I.

But something seems to have gone wrong in the last few decades, and I am not the only one who has noticed. We live today in a world where women's reproductive rights are threatened; where in many countries, women are subjected in their teens to the barbaric ritual of genital circumcision; where innocent young men and women die fighting in wars we should never have entered, while rich corporations and blockheaded politicians profit in terms of money, power, or both. It is a world where many people still live not only below the poverty line but below the minimum daily needs of sustenance.

My response to this was, in 2005, to make a pledge to the global Millennium Village Initiative, which was commissioned by the United Nations in 2002 to develop a plan to reverse grinding poverty, hunger, and disease. The idea is that impoverished villages can transform themselves if they are empowered through investments in practical technologies for health, food production, education, access to clean water, and essential infrastructure. My $1,050,000 private donation (over three years, 2006 through 2008) to this effort has gone to alleviate problems and provide sustainable living in at least two African villages, Ikarum and Ibarum, in Ondo Province, Nigeria. My gift was enhanced by UN and Ondo provincial government contributions, so it had a greater impact.

I was inspired to take this action by Professor Jeffrey Sachs, who wrote *The End of Poverty* (a wonderful book that was not published by SAGE). I bought it in a local bookstore early in 2005, read it quickly (it is short and a great read), and was moved to act. Later that year, I announced my commitment. I believed then, as I believe now, that such a project is a plan worth trying. Since then, in three short years, we have seen this approach begin to work very effectively in the Ondo Province of Nigeria (as it had worked in over 100 other African villages by the time I completed my gift). By making this donation and taking such a stand, I publicly challenged the leadership of the American government to contribute the promised .07% of our GNP to foreign aid to the UN via Dr. Sachs's Earth Institute at Columbia University, to end famine around the world in 25 years—not 50 years. This is actually a promise our government made in 1995 in a series of conferences on International Millennium Goals, many of them designed to help solve this problem under the aegis of the United Nations.

Unfortunately, that promise by our government has not been kept, and I wonder, *Will it be kept any time soon?* Frankly, with the wars in Iraq and Afghanistan, I doubt it. Terrorism, bombs—there's always a good excuse. But I still care, and I want to be sure that somehow we as a nation keep our promise. I am committed to doing my part, and I ask others I know to do theirs. I owe it to my conscience, my children, my grandchildren, and now my great-grandchildren to leave behind me a world that has solutions, not just problems, bringing social justice and sustainability to people everywhere.

I believe strongly that there are times when we have to do what we know is right. Sometimes, we have to hold our elected representatives' feet to the fire, to let them know where the heat is *really* coming from. Sometimes we have to stand up and be counted. I firmly believe that if we want to truly support our troops, we need to first end needless dying and bring true democracy, not pseudo-democracy, to wherever possible. We need to give people around the world the four freedoms that Franklin Delano Roosevelt articulated in 1941: *freedom of speech and expression, freedom of religion, freedom from want,* and *freedom from fear.*

I also believe that as a first step to the empowerment of the people who live in the poorer places on our globe, we must encourage sustainable economies. Then we need to encourage those people to take the next steps, and the next, until their voices are heard and their needs are met, and their children are healthy, educated, and able to assist their own towns, villages, cities, and societies. Only then can they move ahead and prosper.

But a first response should—indeed, *must*—be followed up. Decades ago, I found a quotation in *Bartlett's Familiar Quotations* that has meaning for me:

> *We all are blind until we see*
>
> *That in the human plan*
>
> *Nothing is worth the making if*
>
> *It does not make the man.*
>
> *Why build these cities glorious*
>
> *If man* unbuilded goes?*
>
> *In vain we build the world, unless*
>
> *The builder also grows.*
>
> —*Edwin Markham*

---

*Read man as "humanity" even if it doesn't rhyme as well!

We are each, in our own way, builders. We build for our families usually and often for our communities. These days, all communities are linked by the mass media, by dispersed families, by travel, and so forth. So we have strong possibilities and wonderful opportunities to do great things both small and large. It is my belief (and hope) that many of us will use them for humanity.

Caring Matters

During the past 45 years at SAGE Publications, we have published a lot about such important subjects. We will continue to do so, because we care. We, too, have dreams and the belief to sustain those dreams, to turn them into plans and actions.

I would like to thank my colleagues—there are just over 1,000 of them at SAGE Publications, in California, London, India, and now in the Asia-Pacific region—for the hard and smart work that has made our company grow and prosper. I am also very grateful to the thousands of authors, editors, and editorial board members and the scores of scholarly societies that entrust us with the dissemination of their intellectual output. I am very indebted to them for that and also for what they do as individuals and groups every day, every month, and every year. And I salute and acknowledge the work and vision of the tens of thousands of authors we are (and have been) privileged to publish over the decades.

In return, I promise that our company will remain independent and will remain committed to its vision by giving back through both corporate and personal philanthropy. Our employees will continue to give of their time and talent in their own communities. We enjoy our work and take pride in what we do. We believe in education and its contribution to the building of social capital and beneficial social change.

Thank you all for believing in us, and know that we join you in believing and hoping for a better future for humanity.

Sara Miller McCune
Founder and Executive Chairman
SAGE Publications, Inc.

Name Index

Subject Index

About the Author

SARA MILLER McCUNE is the Executive Chairman of SAGE Publications, Inc., as well as President of the McCune Foundation, based in Ventura. In 1965, she founded SAGE Publications in New York City, and moved the company to California in mid-1966, serving as its President for 18 years, prior to becoming SAGE's Executive Chairman in 1984. Ms. McCune also serves as a Director of two of SAGE's most notable affiliates—SAGE Publications, Ltd (London) and Corwin Press, a leading publisher for educational administrators and teachers. SAGE Publications India Pvt. Ltd and SAGE Publications Asia-Pacific Pte. Ltd are other affiliates, founded in 1981 and 2006, respectively. Ms. McCune founded the Miller-McCune Center for Research, Media and Public Policy in Santa Barbara, California in 2007 and currently serves as President. The April/May issue of *Miller-McCune* magazine was published in 2008, with its online counterpart (Miller-McCune.com) debuting at the end of March 2008. The magazine has won five major awards during its first two years. It is now read regularly by over 250,000 people.

Memberships

- Board of Directors of the American Academy of Political and Social Science located in Philadelphia, Pennsylvania.

- University of California Santa Barbara (UCSB) Foundation Board of Trustees (resigned, after over a decade's service, in December 2009) and the UCSB Chancellor's Council.

- Santa Barbara Social Venture Partners as of June 2009, currently serving as a member-at-large on the Executive Committee.

- Former Trustee of the Fielding Graduate University, which is headquartered in Santa Barbara, California, serving as a Board Member for eight years, including the final year as Board Chair. Also, served as Interim President in 1999–2000.

- Board of the Santa Barbara Center for the Performing Arts as member and Chief Financial Officer from 1998 through June 2008. During that period, the Center restored and reopened the historic Granada Theatre in downtown Santa Barbara. Ms. McCune also served as the first Capital Campaign committee chair for more than five years.

- President of the McCune Foundation (a member of the Santa Barbara Foundation Roundtable).

- Past President of the Santa Barbara Foundation Roundtable.

Awards

- 1988—The American Evaluation Association awarded her a Special Award for Distinguished Contributions to the Field of Evaluation, in recognition of the influential role SAGE Publications played in institutionalizing the field of evaluation.

- 1993—The Knowledge Utilization Society awarded her its Outstanding and Distinguished Career Achievement Award (a similar award was given to George D. McCune in Memoriam).

- 1998—The National Society of Fundraising Executives recognized her as the 1998 Philanthropist of the Year for Santa Barbara County.

- 2001—Women's Economic Ventures, a Santa Barbara–based group that sponsors entrepreneurship training for women, honored her with the Trailblazer Award.

- 2002—The Fielding Graduate Institute (now the Fielding Graduate University) recognized her as a Lifetime Fellow.

- 2002—The Anti-Defamation League and the Santa Barbara B'nai B'rith Lodge granted her the Distinguished Community Service Award.

- 2003—Ernst & Young awarded her the Entrepreneur of the Year Award in "Arts and Entertainment" for the Greater Los Angeles area in June. In November 2003, Ernst & Young awarded her the Entrepreneur of the Year Award for the "Spirit of Entrepreneurship" on a national level.

- 2004—The Channel Islands Chapter of the Multiple Sclerosis Society honored her with the Hope Award.

- 2005—The University of California at Santa Barbara Alumni Association named her Honorary Alumna of the Year.

- 2006—Emmaus of Santa Barbara gave her the Pierre Claeyssens Award for Distinguished Service. Emmaus is a local youth organization dedicated to empowering youth to break the cycle of self-destructive behaviors.

- 2006—The *Santa Barbara News Press* awarded her the Lifetime Distinguished Community Service Achievement Award. Her selection was based on the recommendation of previous winners of the award.

- 2007—The State Street Ballet in Santa Barbara named her Annual Honoree.

- 2008—The Santa Barbara Scholarship Foundation named her Santa Barbara Entrepreneur of the Year.

- 2008—The Women's Campaign International (WCI) honored her at an event entitled *Shattering the Glass Ceiling: Honoring Inspirational Women Around the Globe.* Other honorees at the same event included Hillary Rodham Clinton, Katie Couric, and the president of Liberia.

- 2009—The Rotary Club of Santa Barbara presented Sara with the Paul Harris Fellow Award.

- 2009—The *Independent* newspaper named her as one of the "Local Heroes."

- 2010— She was honored with the Shining Star Lifetime Achievement Award (first recipient) at the Santa Barbara Women's Festival.

Ms. McCune is a graduate of Queens College of the City University of New York. She is the stepmother of four, the grandmother of four, and the great-grandmother of three. Ms. McCune resides in Montecito, California.

About the Contributors

STEPHEN BARR was born and raised in the UK, with many happy holidays in Spain, and some years in the United States, since his father was an internationally respected scholar whose work on the Old Testament and the Hebrew language led to frequent lectures as well as teaching positions in the United States. Stephen is a graduate of Oxford University. His work in the publishing industry includes a period at the Open University during an exciting time in its history, and his knowledge of textbook publishing for the college and university market began at this time. In the latter part of 1986, Stephen left the Open University Press and joined SAGE Publications in London. He was initially asked to focus on building the sociology publishing program, along with related disciplines. Gradually Stephen assumed increasing responsibility for London's commissioning team, and by 1988 he was Editorial Director. He became Managing Director of SAGE London in 1996. As SAGE continued its growth in India, and we began planning for SAGE Asia-Pacific, Stephen was asked to do more work internationally. He was a key player in the launch and growth of our operation based in Singapore (which was established in 2006) and recently assumed the title of President of SAGE International for the SAGE group while continuing to serve as Managing Director of SAGE London. Stephen lives in London with his wife, Susan, and their four boys, Adam, Alexander, Theo, and Marcus.

MATTHEW JACKSON is retired and living in Elstree, a suburb of London, with his wife Marian. He served with the Royal Navy during the latter part of World War II, set up a company in the United States importing English confectionary, was a Management Consultant with an extensive list of clients, and was a Fellow of the British Institute of Management. He was also a CEO of a London Hotel Group and has served on various boards of directors, including that of SAGE Publications, London. The Jackson family and the McCune family have been friends and celebrated birthdays, anniversaries, and holidays together for over four decades. Matthew has authored two books, one on the subject of executive recruitment (his area of expertise with the Tack Organisation in the UK) and the other an autobiographical volume titled *Not Only a Grandpa*.

ZIYAD MARAR was born in Baghdad, Iraq, in 1966. He lived in the Middle East until the age of 10 before moving to London, where he now lives. His entire publishing career has been at SAGE, where he has worked for more than 20 years. He holds a B.Sc. degree in psychology (Exeter University) and an M.A. in the philosophy and psychology of language (London University), and he has completed several years of postgraduate research in this field, toward an uncompleted Ph.D. thesis on the structure and content of truth. His ongoing interest in philosophy and psychology has led to him writing books and articles. His first book, *The Happiness Paradox* (2003), reflects his interest in the way philosophy and psychology can contribute to a better understanding of modern identity. His most recent book, *Deception* (2008), looks at our complex relationship with the truth, including tensions that arise from self-deception, the need to be truthful, and the need to be kind. His is currently working on a book on the nature of intimacy. He lives in London with his wife, Kate, and three daughters, Anna, Ellie, and Charlotte.

NANCY MARRIOTT is an editor, author, writing coach, and radio show co-host. Nancy, who assisted me in writing this book, has an M.A. in Teaching of English Literature and Theater Arts from Columbia University and a B.A. in English from the University of Massachusetts. In 1997, she helped Dr. Candace Pert write the best-selling *Molecules of Emotion* (Scribner), and in 2006, she co-authored *Everything You Need to Know to Feel Good* (Hay House) with Dr. Pert. Nancy lives in Santa Barbara, California, with her husband, Richard, and is an adjunct instructor in writing and ESL at Santa Barbara City College.

DAVID McCUNE's interest in social science, social policy, and research first grew during his career as a journalist. Prior to his association with SAGE, Mr. McCune wrote for a variety of newspapers and magazines and for a period was a writer and editor at Time, Inc. Mr. McCune served as president of SAGE from 1988 to 1998 and expanded the company's publishing programs while retaining SAGE's commitment to education. He assembled a team of publishers who share a vision of widespread dissemination of educational books, journals, and software.

Mr. McCune led SAGE into many new areas of educational publishing, including new scholarly disciplines and new educational markets outside SAGE's core academic markets. Among his initiatives was the launching of Corwin Press in 1990, a company devoted to putting practical information in the hands of educational administrators in the PreK–12 market. Today Corwin is a leading source of advice and ideas for school principals, superintendents, and other school administrators, as well as for teachers.

BLAISE SIMQU joined SAGE Publications shortly after completing his master's degree at UCLA, with brief publishing experience at the Hampton-Brown Company. Initially, he was a production editor, and his talent for academic publishing as well as his deep interest in government and politics quickly earned him promotion to acquisitions editor for political science. True love, however, caused him to relocate to San Francisco, where his talents were put to work for Jossey-Bass (a publisher that subsequently became part of Macmillan, which became part of Simon & Schuster, which in turn became acquired by an international giant). Blaise, however, had won his bride long before then and had gone to work for Kinko's Corporation (before it was acquired by FedEx). There he served as the executive liaison between Kinko's and the publishing industry. Knowing that Blaise was once again within reach, the McCunes enticed him back to SAGE as Vice President of our rapidly expanding Journals Division (while his bride, Erin, was happily working at Amgen, our Thousand Oaks neighbor). In 2000, Blaise was promoted to the position of Executive Vice President for the entire Higher Education Group, essentially the book and journal publishing program in the United States. In the summer of 2005, Blaise was appointed as President and CEO. Blaise and Erin are now living in Westlake Village, raising two wonderful children, Isabelle and William.